BROKEN BONDS

A CENTURY FOUNDATION BOOK

BROKEN BONDS

The Existential Crisis of Egypt's
Muslim Brotherhood, 2013–22

Abdelrahman Ayyash | Amr ElAfifi | Noha Ezzat

About The Century Foundation

The Century Foundation is a progressive, independent think tank that conducts research, develops solutions, and drives policy change to make people's lives better. We pursue economic, racial, gender, and disability equity in education, health care, and work, and promote U.S. foreign policy that fosters international cooperation, peace, and security.

Board of Trustees of The Century Foundation

Bradley Abelow
Jonathan Alter
Alexander Morgan Capron, Emeritus
Jacob S. Hacker
Melissa Harris-Perry
John B. King, Jr.

George Miller
Alicia Munnell
Richard Ravitch, Emeritus
Damon A. Silvers
Harvey I. Sloane, M.D., Emeritus

Mark Zuckerman, *President*

Library of Congress Cataloguing-in-Publication Data Available from the publisher upon request.

Manufactured in the United States of America

Cover design by Abigail Grimshaw
Text design by Cynthia Stock

Copyright © 2023 by The Century Foundation, Inc. All rights reserved. No part of this publication may be reproduced, stored in a retrieval system, or transmitted, in any form or by any means, electronic, mechanical, photocopying, recording, or otherwise, without the prior written permission of The Century Foundation.

Contents

Acknowledgments	vii
Prologue: A Personal History from Indoctrination to Alienation, by Abdelrahman Ayyash	1
Part I. An Introduction to the Muslim Brotherhood	15
Part II. The Brotherhood's Three Crises	47
Chapter 1. The Identity Crisis	49
Chapter 2. The Legitimacy Crisis	88
Chapter 3. The Membership Crisis	116
Epilogue: Unvanquished—But No Path to Victory	147
Notes	159

Abdelrahman Ayyash

Abdelrahman Ayyash is a fellow at Century International and director of its Egyptian Muslim Brotherhood working group. He is an award-winning journalist and a researcher specializing in Islamic movements and Middle East Politics. Since 2016, Ayyash has been working as a researcher on Egypt with human rights organizations, including Human Rights Watch and the Freedom Initiative. He has published reports and articles about the Muslim Brotherhood for the Carnegie Endowment for International Peace, the German Council on Foreign Relations (DGAP), the Arab Reform Initiative, and others. Ayyash is a master of public policy candidate at Jackson School of Global Affairs at Yale University.

Amr ElAfifi

Amr ElAfifi is a PhD candidate at Syracuse University where he works on the relationship between trauma and political participation. He is also the research manager at the Freedom Initiative where his work is focused on conditions of detainment and how they affect political prisoners and their loved ones. Prior to these positions, Amr worked at the World Bank where he focused on bettering investment climates in fragile and conflict countries.

Noha Ezzat

Noha Ezzat is a writer and researcher. Her work focuses on geopolitics, and political and historical sociology, with a focus on Egypt, Turkey, and Iran. She holds a master's in International Relations from Durham University with a thesis on war and modernization in Iran. Noha has published research work and articles for Durham University's Institute of Islamic and Middle Eastern Studies, Al Jazeera Center for Studies, Carnegie Endowment for International Peace, and Hungary's Institute for Trade and Foreign Affairs.

Acknowledgments

The project would not have been possible without the generous support of the Henry Luce Foundation, which has enabled a multiyear effort. It was also made possible by the board of trustees and our colleagues at The Century Foundation (TCF), led by Chairman Bradley Abelow and President Mark Zuckerman, who have created the space for Century International to extend its commitment to innovative policy research. Century International's Advisory Board provided critical guidance to the organization: Lina Attalah, Melani Cammett, Mona Fawaz, Michael Wahid Hanna, and Marc Lynch. Luce program director Toby Volkman helped conceive this project, and Jonathan VanAntwerpen helped see it to its conclusion.

First and foremost, we would like to thank our interviewees and participants. Talking about the Muslim Brotherhood in this time period entailed serious security risks, as well as the recollection of the trauma of political violence, exile, and the personal plights of friends and family members. The fact that they spoke with us and introduced us to their friends and colleagues is not something we take for granted. We hope that our treatment of the organization and their stories honors their contributions. In particular, we would like to thank the current members of the Muslim Brotherhood who helped us understand the recent internal situation of the movement.

We also extend our gratitude to a group of incredible reviewers whose feedback has only contributed to making this work better.

These reviewers include Hesham Gaafar, Nathan Brown, Elizabeth Nugent, Heba Raouf Ezzat, and Mohammad Affan. Each of these scholars has inspired our scholarship in their own way, and their feedback on this project is a testament to their ingenuity and expertise. Thanassis Cambanis and Eamon Kircher-Allen at Century International showed a level of grace, brilliance, and trust in the authors and project that we thought was not possible. They were thorough as ever, but gave us the space to think and articulate our ideas. It is because of them that we have the book we wanted to write.

This project would not have been possible if not for the support of our loved ones. Amr ElAfifi would like to thank his wife, Walaa, who has been not only a supportive partner, but a collaborator in many ways on this project. He has ruined many dinners and date nights sharing frustrations about the project. He appreciates her patience and loves her for it and much more. He would also like to thank his father, Ahmed, who he bored endlessly with different details about the book but who, nonetheless, always led with kindness even when he vehemently disagreed. Even though he still thinks Amr should go to law school, he never shies from supporting his work and sharing how proud he is. Amr would also like to thank his father-in-law, Hamed, for offering astute feedback with tremendous generosity and grace, and always emphasizing the importance of thinking methodologically. Last but not least, much thanks go to Yael Zeira, Amr's wonderful dissertation advisor, for her understanding and support as he worked on non-dissertation projects.

Abdelrahman Ayyash would love to thank his wife, Mona. This book came at a time of much personal and professional tribulation. Throughout all of this, she has rolled with the challenges with love, grace, and courage. He would also like to thank his daughter, Dima, who sat in Zoom meetings, slept to the sound of typing, and never failed to brighten a tough moment throughout the project. This, and everything else he does, is always for her.

Noha Ezzat would love to thank her parents, who have shown support and patience as she worked on the book.

Responsibility for any errors rests with the authors alone.

— The authors

Prologue: A Personal History from Indoctrination to Alienation

By Abdelrahman Ayyash

The Muslim Brotherhood has intrigued me for as long as I can remember. In fact, my connection to the Brotherhood began before I was even born: my grandfather was a schoolteacher in his early twenties when he joined the group, a few years after it was founded in 1928 by Hassan al-Banna, another schoolteacher in his early twenties. When I was four years old, I attended my first "meeting," a playdate with several neighborhood boys in a mosque near our home in Mansoura, a Nile Delta city 120 kilometers north of Cairo. For more than sixteen years, I attended countless lectures, fishing and camping trips, movie nights, protests, and political events with the group's members and leaders. During much of this time, I was unaware that the people I was meeting with were members of a political movement with hundreds of thousands of members in Egypt and around the world. Although I attended my last weekly *usra* meeting (literally, family meeting), in December 2010, the Muslim Brotherhood still occupies a considerable chunk of my personal interest, as well as my professional interest as a journalist and a researcher.[1]

The Brotherhood provided a community for me and many other young Egyptians. Some of them grew up to have several forms of attachment to the group, and others rose to be high-ranking members and mid-level leaders. The Muslim Brotherhood gives its members a safe social circle and a livelihood. If you are a member who is also a business owner, a doctor, an accountant, an engineer, or (especially) a lawyer, you are assured of clientele. Along with the benefits of Brotherhood membership come risks: a Brother (in the parlance of the group) knows that he will probably get arrested at some point. He also knows that his family will be well taken care of while he is in detention. The Brotherhood used to provide detainees' families with the same salaries their breadwinners earned before arrest, maintain the lifestyle these families were used to, and even pay for their children's private schools.

The Brotherhood also confers social bonds. Most of Egypt is a conservative society in which strict social and religious norms govern the relationships between men and women. A Brotherhood member can rely on the group to arrange his or his children's marriage (obviously, to other members). Brotherhood parents also rely on the group's network for childcare and support. For many years, the Brotherhood built schools and kindergartens that served the organization and other Egyptians.

No member would describe the Brotherhood as a mere political party, a social movement, or a religious sect. It is none of the above. It is all of the above.

Banna himself told early members that the Brotherhood was a comprehensive organization that had space for a wide array of activities and thoughts.[2] The version of Islam it espoused was comprehensive and did not differentiate between the practicing of politics and of religion. Banna's goal was to form a vanguard of believers to revive the *ummah* (the Muslim nation) and reestablish what he described as Islam's "mastership of the world."[3] Banna intentionally created the all-inclusive support system of the Brotherhood to advance these goals. What Banna did not realize, however, is that the Brotherhood's perquisites would more effectively keep members in the organization than its policies or politics.

When I was a child, no one in the Brotherhood talked to me about politics—only religion and how to be a good Muslim. A good Muslim cares for fellow Muslims; that is why I was first introduced to the concept of ummah when I was just eleven. In the early years of the first decade of this century, the only political issue people talked about was the Palestinian struggle. The Brotherhood produced anthems (*anasheed*) that honored the resilience of Palestinian children and the resistance against the Israeli occupation. In 2001, when I was in fifth grade, I attended my first vigil after Friday prayers in the mosque near my home for Palestinian children killed in Israeli attacks on Gaza. Protests in support of the Palestinian Intifada were raging across Egyptian schools and universities.

The anger about Israel's actions was sincere and organic, but what I didn't know, as an eleven-year-old, was that it also served a political purpose for the regime of Hosni Mubarak, which allowed such demonstrations to release the pressure caused by its mounting political and economic failures. But even though Mubarak may have viewed the movement against Israel's excesses as a welcome distraction, it was also a founding moment in the collaboration between different political actors—an antecedent of the coalitions that ultimately led to his ouster in the 2011 revolution.

The U.S. invasion of Iraq in 2003, when I was thirteen, was another moment that brought diverse groups together. In fact, I attended my first significant protest that year, against the invasion. Once again, Mubarak's regime supported the protest and provided it with a venue, the Mansoura sports stadium. Tens of thousands of protesters from the Brotherhood, political parties, leftist movements, and other labor and professional unions filled the stands while I walked with other young Brothers on the track, carrying empty coffins with messages on them; mine said "Freedom." I felt great pride knowing my father was watching from the stands. The protest was all that we talked about for days. Baghdad fell into the hands of U.S. soldiers that week.

But the political aspect of the organization was not a priority for Brotherhood members. In our weekly usra meetings after the invasion of Iraq, my Brotherhood mentor talked about our changing bodies and how we could be good Muslims by "lowering our gazes"—a religious term meaning to avoid looking at women, let alone "indecent" photos and videos.

But the Brotherhood soon took a turn that made it more relevant for Egyptian politics—and more political for me.

In 2004, the Brotherhood's highest executive entity, the Guidance Bureau, made a decision known internally as the "identity declaration": it would start using the name of the Muslim Brotherhood publicly. Until then, Brotherhood affiliates had been using aliases. The Brotherhood's university students, for example, called themselves the "Students of the Islamic Current." Of course, Egyptian authorities knew that they were affiliated with the Brotherhood, but using a different name kept the appearance of an organization that didn't have overt Egyptian political ambitions. Following the identity declaration, however, these students' pamphlets were signed by "Students of the Muslim Brotherhood."[4]

Around the same time, the Brotherhood began making good use of the Internet. Young members led in the adoption of these new communications technologies, whose adoption in the Brotherhood had initially been slow. A computer-savvy Brotherhood mentor, Abdelhameed Abdelfattah, helped me create my first email account. (The government executed Abdelfattah in 2019, after a flawed, unfair trial.)[5] I used this account to access ikhwan.net, the first forum for the Muslim Brotherhood on the Web. The site, which is now defunct, was not exactly a bastion of free speech—admins had strict morality rules, monitored private messages, removed foul language, and watered down jokes between male and female members.

Still, it represented a major advance in the ability of Brotherhood members in Egypt and abroad to exchange ideas.

In 2005, the Brotherhood ran for the parliamentary elections. I campaigned for the two Brotherhood candidates in my hometown, and for the first time, I visited areas that I had not known existed in my small city. With other Brotherhood members, I marched in the street to campaign in Mansoura's poorer districts, where residents pumped their fists in support, pledged to vote for the Brotherhood's candidates, or prayed for them in soft voices.

The government did not repress the campaign's marches, though thugs (paid for by the ruling party's candidates) attacked Brotherhood representatives and supporters on election day. In one such attack that I witnessed, a Brotherhood member standing next to me recognized one of the attackers. "I know this person," he said, shocked. "The Brotherhood has been supporting his family for years." The incident remains vivid for me because it underlined that, while the Brotherhood served millions of Egyptians with its social solidarity programs, those beneficiaries were often not aware of, let alone committed to, the group's politics and ideology.

The Muslim Brotherhood won 88 out of 444 seats in the lower chamber of parliament, and the organization celebrated the dawning of a new era in relations between the group and the regime. But this was not to be. In January 2006, Hamas—an offshoot of the Brotherhood founded two decades earlier in Gaza—won a majority in elections in the Palestinian Territories, and tried but failed to form a coalition government.[6] Hamas's victory showed the appeal of Islamists throughout the region.[7] But it also alarmed many in foreign policy circles in the Middle East and beyond, which in turn gave Mubarak's regime an excuse to crack down on the Brotherhood in Egypt. In December 2006, the Egyptian security forces arrested thirty or so leaders of the Muslim Brotherhood, including its deputy chairman, Khairat al-Shater, who was believed to have engineered the group's electoral victory.

Around this time, I started writing a blog on my daily life, which necessarily meant writing about the Brotherhood. My audience grew quickly because I offered a rare glimpse into the organization. Journalists from the opposition and independent newspapers regarded me and a small group of bloggers as representing the "third generation of the Muslim Brotherhood." People were interested in knowing more about personal aspects of members' lives that had not been publicly discussed before. The readers loved how Brotherhood bloggers shared not only behind-the-scenes organizational matters, but also their movie recommendations, their amateur poems, and their love stories. Journalists started asking Brotherhood leaders for comments on what I and other bloggers wrote, which included our thoughts about the Brotherhood, and our differences with the group on social issues such as listening to music or watching movies (acts the Brotherhood frowned upon). Without even realizing it, we were humanizing the Muslim Brotherhood. The leadership, however, did not like what its "third generation" was doing. Many Brotherhood leaders thought of us as rebellious youth with shallow roots in the organization.[8] And it was true that most of us did not have high formal ranks in the Brotherhood, which has a complex and carefully managed hierarchy.

However, a few leaders saw the Brotherhood blogosphere as an opportunity to refresh the group. In 2007, Khaled Hamza, a Brotherhood media guru, asked me to work under him at ikhwanweb.com, the official English-language Brotherhood website, for the campaign against referring civilians to military trials. Shater and other Brotherhood leaders had just been referred to military trials, and the Brotherhood mobilized human rights advocates, civil society organizations, and Islamic scholars worldwide to denounce these trials. I was just seventeen, and over the moon to meet Ramsey Clark—a controversial figure and prominent critic of US foreign policy and the former U.S. attorney general—upon his arrival to Egypt to support the

Brotherhood's cause by monitoring the trial (which Egyptian authorities banned him from attending).[9]

The campaign successfully attracted civil society's attention to the calamity befalling the Brotherhood. But it also shone an uncomfortable spotlight on some of the group's more controversial ideas, which were articulated that year in its first-ever party platform.[10] Some of these ideas, such as a proposal to create an elected council of religious scholars to review legislation, and the disqualification of women and Christians from the state presidency and premiership, also created significant discord within the Brotherhood. I disagreed with them strongly, and wrote blog posts criticizing the platform, which were picked up by the national media. Brotherhood leadership took note, and in October, Mohamed Morsi—then a member of the group's Guidance Bureau and the head of its political committee—summoned me to his office.

I told several Brotherhood bloggers and young members about the proposed meeting. A dozen of them, including two women bloggers, came to the meeting held one evening in late October at the Brotherhood's parliamentary bloc headquarters in Cairo.

After the sunset prayer, which Morsi led (as the presiding imam), he talked for nearly forty minutes about the Muslim Brotherhood's ideology and work methods. The speech was so general and out of touch with our concerns that one of the two women walked out before Morsi even finished. Ironically, she became one of Morsi's aides when he was president in 2012. Morsi then opened the floor for comments and questions—and he got an earful. Most of the questions revolved around the weak roles of youth and women in the organization, the idea of separating the Brotherhood's preaching from its politics, and the party platform. Morsi appeared to listen attentively, but his answers were just as shallow and disconnected as his initial remarks. "This is how the Brotherhood understands Islam," he told us, defending the Brotherhood's position on the ineligibility of women and Christians to hold the presidency or premiership. "If you have other preferences, the space is open [for you to leave the Brotherhood and join other groups]. Egypt needs your effort and energy."

The meeting was the first time I thought about leaving the Brotherhood, but the reality was unlike what Morsi said; the "space" was not open, and practicing politics outside the Brotherhood meant that I either joined Mubarak's party or one of the shabby opposition parties, which I would have never done. Sooner or later, however, all of the participants in that meeting left the Muslim Brotherhood. One, Mohammed Adel, cofounded, a few months later, one of the most prominent political movements in Egypt's recent history: the April 6 Youth Movement, named after the date in 2008 that workers in the industrial city of al-Mahalla al-Kubra in the Nile Delta went on strike.[11]

The call for a general strike attracted professional syndicates and unions, political parties, and prominent individuals, but not the Muslim Brotherhood. The Brotherhood rejected the call to participate, saying they did not "know the people behind it," and asked their members not to interact with such calls.[12] As a blogger and activist, I openly supported strike calls and tried to spread the word within my Brotherhood circles. Along with a group of university colleagues, I had a meeting with a local Brotherhood leader in Mansoura at which he recited quotes from Banna that dismissed the idea of revolution. He told us that the Brotherhood could not ethically justify the calls for a general strike: "If we are to support a strike in Egypt, how would we react to similar calls against Hamas in Gaza? We should teach the people to be patient and not revolt because of economic hardships." In that moment, it became clear to me that the Muslim Brotherhood was, at heart, a counterrevolutionary organization.

Such ideas were being discussed among groups of activists and researchers, and this is when I met my coauthor Noha Khaled for the first time. I saw Noha in 2009 on the margins of an initiative that was founded by university students organizing monthly lectures on history, politics, and religion, and our work continued to intersect thereafter. During her undergraduate years, she participated in student activities dedicated to politics, and after the eruption of the 2011 uprising, she joined the presidential campaign of Abdel Moneim Aboul Fotouh in 2012. Afterward, her work spanned education, media, publishing, and academic research, and upon completing her master's at Durham University, she specialized in the political and historical sociology of the Middle East.

Noha's work dealt with the central role of religion in social and political organization, and how this role affected the institutions of the modern state in the region, particularly Egypt, Turkey, and Iran. Her area of expertise was helpful in crafting a sociological framework for this research, as it situated the Brotherhood within the larger context of Egyptian politics and society; it shed light on the dilemmas impacting the state and the Brotherhood at once—which are usually overlooked in short-term policy-oriented studies.

I officially left the Muslim Brotherhood in 2010. The years that followed saw the 2011 revolution that deposed Mubarak, the short-lived and inept presidency of Morsi, the recapture of the Egyptian state by the authoritarian forces of Abdel Fattah el-Sisi, and the slaughter of some nine hundred Brotherhood supporters in the Rabaa Massacre of August 14, 2013.

I left Egypt one day after the military coup of July 2013, and have been unable to return since. I ended up in Turkey, where I worked for humanitarian organizations supporting Syrian refugees. I then worked as a journalist, focusing on issues of the Muslim Brotherhood and democratization in Egypt. In 2016, I met my coauthor Amr ElAfifi in Istanbul, where he was writing about perceptions of state violence across different social and political groups in Egypt. Upon finishing his bachelor's, his work and research often intersected with themes close to political violence and its aftermath. At the World Bank, he worked on fragile states and countries in conflict, primarily focusing on bettering the business environment in the aftermath of conflict.

This work coincided with his involvement with the Freedom Initiative, an organization dedicated to conducting research on and advocating for political prisoners in Egypt. In this role, Amr interacted with detainees, former detainees, and families of detainees. Given the widespread arrests of Brotherhood members, he came to interact with a sizable number of both members and former members. Beyond human rights research, Amr's dissertation work looks at the political consequences of trauma and victimization among post-Arab Spring populations. His research provided an excellent launchpad for this project, because it focused on the lived experiences of members who had endured many forms and incidents of victimization.

Today, the leaders and members of the Egyptian Muslim Brotherhood are scattered, principally in Turkey (where there are at least 15,000), but also in countries in the Gulf, in Sudan, and elsewhere. The organization is fractured and somewhat adrift—more so than it has been at any point in its ninety-four-year history, packed as that history has been with state repression. In this book, Noha, Amr, and I attempt to show how the modern world's most influential Islamic organization arrived at this point of existential crisis, and where it might go next.

Our personal history, necessarily, informs this analysis—and shows that, as devastating as the last decade of authoritarian resurgence has been for the Brotherhood, the cracks that have nearly riven it apart today began showing much earlier. Our generation grew up believing in the vision of the Muslim Brotherhood and discovered a reality that fell well short of the ideal.

In the years that preceded 2011, Egyptian intellectuals enthusiastically debated scholarship that anticipated the eclipse of "political Islam." A diverse array of scholars, including Asef Bayat, Gilles Kepel, and Olivier Roy, imagined a post-Islamism world in which

Islamists would abandon idealism for pragmatism, leaving their organizations for "non-movements."[13] According to this perspective, Islamists were retreating from the public sphere to focus on personal religiosity—or they were simply no longer relevant. Less than a decade after these scholars published their ideas, Islamists, in their varying colors, have become major players that gained the votes of tens of millions and have a massive influence on contemporary politics in many Arab countries. This book shows that Islamic social and political formations are not only alive and kicking, but that they may also still be able to influence the region's present and future.

On one hand, the Muslim Brotherhood is arguably the only organization that has been able to maintain a constituency as far back as the monarchy in Egypt. Most other political actors—even those who represented national liberation, drafted the 1923 constitution, or fought against the British colonists—have withered because they were incapable of retaining members or a constituency. Such actors include the Wafd Party (a liberal nationalist party founded in 1918), which now has a weak presence in politics and public discourse, not only because it failed in its negotiations with the British occupation (1882–1956), but because it represented a social and political class that the 1952 coup made less relevant. The Muslim Brotherhood came to represent the aspirations of a class that is not represented either by the state or other actors in Egyptian politics. The organization's religious rhetoric and organizational reach represent a promise of citizenship that is embedded within mainstream religious discourse, and a program of public goods provision that substantiates these claims. The repressive political environment, particularly since the establishment of the republic in 1952, and lack of a free and fair parliamentary and associational life, have rendered the Brotherhood more representative of the Egyptian people than the state or any other group or party. No other current or former political actor or group in Egypt has come close: not the military; nor Anwar Sadat and Mubarak's now defunct National Democratic Party; nor any version of political party that Abdel Fattah el-Sisi has created (such as the Nation's Future Party or the newly founded Egypt-October Party). So, while the Brotherhood may be shaken and its leadership in exile, it is premature to declare that it is over or irrelevant in Egypt—at least until another mechanism or party emerges that is similarly representative.

This book highlights how the Muslim Brotherhood, as an organization and as a social and political movement, is facing the worst crackdown in its history, and how its internal dynamics are shaping the future of the movement. The ultimate adaptability of the Muslim Brotherhood is another characteristic that we try to dissect and understand, in order to explain why it is too early to write an obituary for a movement whose most active members are either behind bars or living in unforgiving exile.

PART I
An Introduction to the Muslim Brotherhood

On June 17, 2019, Mohamed Morsi, Egypt's first democratically elected president and a member of the Brotherhood, fell dead in a Cairo court. After years of near-total isolation and medical negligence, he lay in the courthouse for some time before the presiding judge, Mohammed Shereen Fahmy, ordered an ambulance.[1] Two years later, on July 29, 2022, Ibrahim Munir, the interim general guide of the Brotherhood, told Reuters that the Muslim Brotherhood would not compete for any political positions in Egypt.[2]

The two years following Morsi's death had been consequential. The Brotherhood's support—both domestically and internationally—had dwindled. With Morsi gone, countries that had hosted the Brotherhood for years accelerated steps (which may have been inevitable) to warm to the Egyptian government and turn against the organization. Both Turkey and Qatar resumed relations with Egypt to some extent, and asked Brotherhood members and leaders to leave.

Today, an organization that has successfully adapted to decades of repression is being pushed to the limits of its adaptability—and perhaps its utility.

In an interview we conducted with Munir shortly before his death in November 2022, we asked how the organization conceived of its political trajectory amid changing regional and global dynamics. Munir responded by referring to verses in the Quran in which God tells Moses' mother to "cast him in the river and not worry."[3] We understood Munir to mean that his movement ought to do what it believes is right—by maintaining its ideological and religious beliefs and its peaceful opposition to the government—and not worry about the results. It is hard to ascertain how serious Munir's fatalism was, or whether he was posturing. But what is clear is that, years after being forced to become a transnational organization because of its leadership's expulsion from Egypt, the Brotherhood is now at an even more complex crossroads. Its old strategies for managing its relationship with the Egyptian state, and maintaining a quasi-clandestine presence in Egypt, are no longer relevant. To weather this new crisis, the Brotherhood is being forced to rethink its strategies—and it must do so in the absence of the vast majority of top cadres, who are either in exile, dead, or in jail.

The Muslim Brotherhood has been misunderstood as a political, ideological, or even military organization. But we argue, based on our reading of Muslim Brotherhood history over the last decade, that the organization is properly understood as an elite social organization, with a small but deeply committed membership. We argue that the organization itself misunderstood its own nature, mistakenly believing that in an open competitive political environment the Brotherhood would manifest as an ideological organization with mass mobilizing capability. To the contrary, the chain of events from the Egyptian revolution of January 2011 to the exiled Muslim Brotherhood's internal administrative rifts in 2022 reveals an organization of elite cadres more embedded in a social milieu than in a political or ideological project.

In many ways, studying the Muslim Brotherhood is a study of how autocratic regimes affect social movements and how these movements survive under different waves of repression. It tells us how the scars of these crackdowns and the survival mechanisms they develop come into play in their day-to-day operations as an organization. The Egyptian government's 2013 crackdowns and the subsequent exiles provided a new wave of challenges that gave us an opportunity to peek into the Muslim Brotherhood as an organization.

In this book, we study the changes the Muslim Brotherhood went through in the period between 2013 and 2022 to understand whether and how the organization has changed in this period. To do so, we relied on expert interviews, interviews with senior, junior, and former members of the organization, written and recorded memoirs and interviews, organizational documents, and primary and secondary literature.

Overall, we posit that the organization suffers from three main crises and challenges that, while exacerbated by the 2013 crackdown, were not necessarily caused by it: an identity crisis, a legitimacy crisis, and a membership crisis. The lines between these crises are porous, but we think that they summarize the most pressing challenges the organization is currently facing. Historically, the Brotherhood relied on the centrality of the Cairo office and a cohort of leaders—and the legitimacy they projected—to nip crises in the bud. But with senior leaders and most active members detained, the Brotherhood detached from its organic roots, and the changing nature of the security threats it now faces, the tools that the organization developed to keep itself intact (or even expand) are now contributing to its breakdown.

Part I of this book contains an introduction to the Brotherhood and its history. The core of our analyses and arguments of the post-2013 organization is in Part II, which is organized into three chapters around the Brotherhood's three main crises.

Chapter 1 discusses the Brotherhood's identity crisis, highlighting the organization's historical development and how it morphed under different waves of repression and changing political contexts. Starting with the establishment of the organization by Hassan al-Banna in 1928, the chapter traces critical junctures at which the Brotherhood responded to social and political changes. The organization began to honor the survivors of the repressive crackdowns of Gamal Abdel Nasser (president 1956–70) with promotions and by deferring to their ideology. In the early days of Anwar Sadat (president 1970–81), the political atmosphere in Egypt was relatively more open. At the same time, the population grew exponentially and was increasingly educated. The Brotherhood morphed into a large social organization no less consequential for stability than the state—and yet without being allowed to formally contest politics. In the three decades of Hosni Mubarak's rule (1981–2011), the Brotherhood contended with a public that, for the first time, had internalized much of its rhetoric but had not become members. As the repression against the Brotherhood grew, it seemed more logical to its leaders to protect the social organization they had already built than to pursue political ambition that could cost them dearly. Ultimately, the Brotherhood did fully achieve its apolitical aims and became a social success story. But those successes were not nearly enough to put it in a viable position in a post-2011 landscape.

Chapter 2 discusses the Brotherhood's legitimacy crisis by presenting accounts of the 2013 crackdown and how the Brotherhood, as an organization, contended with its leadership vacuum. Based on several interviews with current and former leaders and members of the Muslim Brotherhood, the chapter analyzes the power struggles within the movement and how it attempted to answer the questions of violence, its international presence, and the internal splits over power and resources. The chapter details the different views of the competing factions within the Brotherhood's leadership, and how one faction managed to control the group through a complex set of ideological, financial, and organizational moves.

Chapter 3 discusses the Brotherhood's membership crisis—the exodus of active members from its ranks. The chapter builds on interviews with current and former members of the Brotherhood. We asked about the lived experience of being a Brother or Sister in the aftermath of the Rabaa Massacre of August 2013, including in the exile that followed. This membership crisis has two main facets. First, the organization is unable to provide for a generation of members in the same way that it has for previous generations. And second, the members themselves are undergoing a series of overlapping and continuing crises posed by both the Brotherhood and the Sisi regime.

In many ways, the membership crisis is an outcome of the crises of identity and legitimacy. People have left the organization for a variety of reasons. Some say the Brotherhood is "not being *brotherhood* enough." Others have lost trust in the leadership. Some left because they are more ideological than the Brotherhood; others because they found the Brotherhood to be too ideological. In our interviews we found that the larger structural challenges the Brotherhood struggled with also affected rank-and-file members. When the organization contended with the leadership vacuum, members lacked overarching strategies of resistance against the government. When the organization contended with the question of whether to embrace or reject violent methods, members fell on either side of a debate that was triggered by their heartbreak and trauma in the aftermath of the Rabaa Massacre. And as the organization tried to co-opt and even coerce different factions, members lost faith that leaders had their best interests at heart.

A Preamble to Studying the Brotherhood

This book does not revisit or question everything we know about the Brotherhood. However, the intervention it makes stems from a critical analysis of some of the ways in which the organization has been discussed and studied, particularly in the aftermath of the War on Terror. Many researchers start their analysis with the moment of the Brotherhood's foundation in March 1928 by Hassan al-Banna, a charismatic twenty-two-year-old teacher in the city of Ismailia on the Suez Canal. Scholars also tend to attribute the movement's foundation to the fall of the Ottoman Empire (or caliphate) only four years earlier. This narrative usually makes it difficult for many, including seasoned readers of Egyptian history, to understand the intellectual and historical roots of the Muslim Brotherhood.

    This popular narrative severs the Muslim Brotherhood—whether deliberately or not—as a religious, social, or even military organization, from the political and socioeconomic contexts of the time of its inception. In doing so, the account not only lacks accuracy, but also negatively affects the quality of the research of the movement's current actions and decisions. To really understand the founding moment of the Muslim Brotherhood, which is one of the most influential schools of thought in the world, one should attempt to comprehend not only the religious and political discourses of the 1920s and the previous decades, but also the major questions of that time, namely those around British colonization and national independence.

It is important to note that the Brotherhood is moved by competing motivations. While some members prioritize self-interest, others mediate their preferences through perceptions of religious commitment and obligations. To be a Brotherhood member in Egypt, under successive repressive governments, is to make yourself vulnerable to job insecurity (as state security intervenes to fire you or halt promotions), surveillance, arrest, torture, and death. Members who join and commit do so for a wide array of reasons, including deep-rooted belief in Islam as something that belongs within the public sphere. Many members dedicate their lives to their communities, and their actions cannot be seen as pursuits of such a narrow perception of self-interest as found in a rational-actor model. Neither can these actions be explained as completely altruistic and in pursuit of God's mercy and heaven. Religion conditions members' experiences, as does the larger political context. Neither are deterministic. Members have sacrificed educational and professional opportunities for the sake of the organization.

Additionally, understanding the Muslim Brotherhood requires a deep understanding of Islam as a religion. To that end, it is important to dissect much of the terminology linked to this study. Throughout this book, we resort to the terms "Islamists" and "Islamism" only when no better alternative vocabulary is possible. In general, these terms are inaccurate; they are also not particularly useful, even if some people refer to themselves as such. These terms are often used in contrast to secular or civil groups and parties (*al-quwa wal-harakat al-islamiyya* versus *al-quwa wal-harakat al-madaniyya*). These demarcations belong to a political and security context that speaks to how the state may view these actors.

In Egypt, a variety of Islamic movements described themselves as Islamist by the 1970s, from Salafi groups and the Brotherhood to al-Gama'a al-Islamiyya (the Islamic Group), which was focused on armed militancy. Usually, however, the term "Islamist" was used as a negative descriptor by outsiders, to contrast Islamists with those of a secular orientation, in particular. By the time of the 2011 uprising, the label had almost no meaning, and was very rarely used by movements to describe themselves. Egypt's state had shed much of its past secularism; the constitution drew on Islamic references, and Egypt's Christian minority suffered discrimination at the hands of secular authorities and religious communities alike. In this book, we at times refer to the Islamic religious movements as a sector, but we aim to be precise and specify which movements and constituents we are referring to.

Many policy-oriented researchers who have addressed the issue of Islamists or Islamic movements in Europe and the United States view Islam as an independent factor of radicalization. For them, the more *Islamic* a movement is, the more violent and fanatic its followers tend to be. This discourse gained momentum after 9/11 among both policy analysts and policymakers. The claim that "Islam is not a religion, but a political movement" spread from right-wing mouthpieces, think tanks, and research institutions to inform U.S. policy. One of the most absurd outcomes of this view was Donald Trump's infamous "Muslim ban," which blocked travel from a variety of Muslim-majority countries while giving preferential treatment to non-Muslim refugees from those countries.[4] This understanding of Islam is inaccurate and counterproductive when it comes to dealing with a religion that has more than 1.8 billion followers around the world. By extension, the approach of studying Islamic movements based on these presumptions is not only an ignorant, discriminatory, and racist one, but also lacks the basic tools to deal with such complex phenomena.

Needless to say, many studies on the behavior of *Islamists* often tackle the issue of the Brotherhood by posing questions about Islam itself. As the Egyptian writer Hesham Gaafar puts it, "the obsession with Islamism as a phenomenon created a mindset that led to posing questions about 'Islam and democracy, Islam and human rights, etc.'"[5] The framing that Gaafar describes reflects a faulty understanding of Islam and Islamism, which assumes that the Islamists' interpretation of Islam *defines* Islam. It also neglects the fact that any religious phenomenon does not only constitute a religion, but also its interpretations, its followers, and their social, economic, and historical contexts, as well as the institutions and organizations that turn religious ideas into discourses for public consumption. Much research has mistaken the forest for the trees. Nothing is inherently *Islamic* despite organizational rhetoric. More importantly, people are not solely motivated by ideology, which is itself a product of societal dynamics that are larger than the sum of their parts. In the case of the Muslim Brotherhood, for example, many right-wing politicians and lobbyists in the United States have been tirelessly advocating for the designation of the movement as a terrorist organization. It has been widely known that most of these efforts are supported and paid for by regional powers, particularly Saudi Arabia and the United Arab Emirates, which see an existential threat in the rise of the Muslim Brotherhood as a political force.[6] Undoubtedly, some of these efforts stem from a genuine fear of the group's ideology and actions. However, a proper understanding of Islam as a religion should right-size these fears: Islam comprises the beliefs of its followers, the different interpretations of its texts, and the contradictions between the many of schools of thought that rely on its scripture for guidance and inspiration.

Still, one does not need to be an expert on Islam to criticize the Muslim Brotherhood or study the group. On one hand, there are a plethora of non-Muslim experts on the movement whose studies and work have guided us through this research, some of whom have produced the most important work on Islamic movements. On the other hand, being Muslim does not mean that the research produced is of the objectiveness or quality that allows for a better understanding of Islamic movements. Arab and Muslim researchers often rely on the same simplistic mindset, core values, and policy concerns that are popular in the West when discussing Islamic movements. This is emblematic in the wide use of the term "political Islam," which became a definitive term for a wide spectrum of ideologies and schools of thought that have nothing in common but their reliance on the main Islamic texts for guidance. The term could not have been coined by someone who is familiar with Islam as a religion, the history of Islamic thought, and the concepts that inform the Islamic movements' ideologies and texts. Although we have used "political Islam" in very few places in this book for the lack of a better term, we are aware that it does not hold explanatory power on its own and could mislead the analysis of serious researchers and policymakers. It is safe to say that the use of the term "Islamism" has become more of a tell about an author's orientation toward a group than an accurate description with a specific referent. Our own study shows the many ways that the Muslim Brotherhood transformed over a decade during which its religiosity (or "Islamism") remained constant, making clear that Islamism offers no explanatory power for the organization's trajectory.

Moreover, while previous studies have often looked at the "Muslim" part of the Muslim Brotherhood, and what that means for its politics, in this book we decidedly focus on the "Brotherhood" side of things. The interactions between members and their leaders, the sense of fraternity among the rank and file, and the followers' feeling of being part of an extended family that provides security and support are more important to our analysis than religion. Factoring in this unquantifiable information leads to better understanding of the group's internal dynamics and decision-making processes. Discussing the Muslim Brotherhood's inception and evolution, taking into account these factors and concerns, can provide us with a clearer idea of what the group stands for, as well as humanize the members' experiences.

Scholarship and research on the Muslim Brotherhood suffer from gaps and, in some cases, ideological distortion. Academic research has thoroughly covered some key periods of the Brotherhood, although there have not been many adequate studies of the Brotherhood's interaction with its context and membership. A great deal of contemporary research into the Brotherhood has been produced by think tanks and government-supported research institutes; much of this work lacks rigor and often takes the form of an advocacy brief against the organization, rather than a serious effort to understand it. Other work, typically financed and sponsored by governmental entities, has used simplistic tools to analyze the Brotherhood in very binary terms in relation to its positions on violence, democracy, women's rights, jihad, and other hot-button issues. One strain of literature has seen the complexity of the Brotherhood experience falling into reductionist traps of Countering Violent Extremism (CVE) programs—a framework that never gained traction with scholars and which is increasingly being set aside by the government agencies that popularized it. These writers amass "data" in the form of interviews or screenshots of Facebook posts, and proceed to analyze these tools with the eyes and tools of security and risk analysts. This includes work done by Eric Trager, Samuel Tadros, Lorenzo Vidino, Mokhtar Awad, Ed Husain, Maajid Nawaz, and Gilles Kepel.[7] This work not only often lacks depth and insight, but has been used in policy circles to dehumanize millions of people and pursue anti-democratic outcomes. If the past twelve years are any indicator, their thoughts about the Muslim Brotherhood were at best misplaced, or gravely mistaken at worst.

More productive and thoughtful work on the Brotherhood has been carried out by scholars including Nathan Brown, Peter Mandaville, Marc Lynch, Khalil al-Anani, Elizabeth Nugent, Steven Brooke, Marie Vannetzel, Ioana Emy Matesan, Victor Willi, and Mohammad Affan.[8] This work is characterized by an exploration of the movement as one situated within a larger sociopolitical context that shapes and reshapes both the organization and its members. Although it often includes harsh criticism of the Muslim Brotherhood's policies and ideology, it does not consider Brotherhood members to be ticking time bombs.

It should be noted that we rely on literature about the Brotherhood in its original Arabic that is unfortunately not yet translated. This includes brilliant work by Hossam Tamam, Abdullah al-Nafisi, Hesham Gaafar, Yasser Fathy, Ammar Fayed, Mohammed Naeem, and many others.[9]

This research effort, which rests on the understanding that the Muslim Brotherhood continues to be relevant for making sense of and predicting the evolution of politics in contemporary Egypt, aims to assess how the organization stands today under its current leadership. This generation is largely composed of those who were released from prison or emerged as activists in the previous decades, and who continue to hold sway over the younger generations and the organization, along with splinter groups. The book also aims to draw a picture that may help its readers envisage how a new generation of the Muslim Brotherhood, some of whom spoke with us throughout this research, will behave at the helm of the Brotherhood or any offshoot groupings that emerge from its umbrella. Such inferences will be especially useful if any of this younger generation comes to exercise political influence in the near future, or if the mother organization returns to the political arena (which may seem unlikely, but is not impossible).

This book neither provides a historical analysis of the decades that preceded the foundation of the Muslim Brotherhood, nor does it attempt to clarify misconceptions about Islam. What it does attempt to do is illuminate the Muslim Brotherhood's rationale, which has long been known only to its members, and particularly its senior members. It provides an analytical framework and a way of thinking through which we can understand the inner workings and trends of the Muslim Brotherhood. This understanding, based on structural analysis and ethnographic work, can provide a springboard for further research on the Brotherhood, in Egypt or elsewhere.

A Short History of the Egyptian Muslim Brotherhood

Hassan al-Banna was thirteen years old when the Egyptian revolution of 1919 erupted against the British occupation. As a school student, Banna took part in student strikes and protests, and wrote passionate poems to support the revolution and its calls for national independence. Banna had studied Islam and memorized Quran at a very early age. He later joined the School of Teachers, and then studied the Arabic language and Islam at Dar al-Ulum Faculty in Cairo, graduating in 1927.

The political parties and movements calling for independence in Egypt spanned the ideological spectrum, but not one of them used an Islamic motto to advocate for their ideas. There was one main reason for the absence of Islamic slogans, according to historian Tarek al-Bishri: All popular movements in Egypt, in one way or another, took part in Islamic rhetoric, including the liberal parties such as the Wafd, which effectively led the national independence movement from the early 1920s until the late 1940s.[10] Most of these mainstream movements never questioned the idea of having a connection to the Islamic collective of nations. This is not to say that there was no opposition to the Ottoman policies in Egypt in the nineteenth century on the basis of the empire's Islamic nature, but the opposition to the Ottoman politics in the region was part of a reformist trend throughout the empire, and not a way of seceding from it. In his important work *The Political Movement in Egypt (1945–1953)*, Bishri quotes Mohammed Shafiq Gherbal, another Egyptian historian, asserting that "the mission of Mehmet Ali in the wake of the nineteenth century in Egypt was not to split from the Ottoman Caliphate but to 'revive Ottoman power in a new form.'"[11]

The opposition to the Ottomans in Egypt in the second half of the nineteenth century was an opposition to the policies of the state, and not to the state as a union of nations. The later failure of the Ottomans to support Egypt in the 1880s against the British occupation led the Egyptians to reject the circumstances that led to this occupation—ineffectual Ottoman tutelage—but did not lead to the rejection of the idea of an Islamic union that the Ottomans represented.[12] Evidently, the national movement in Egypt did not grow apart from the Ottoman model, even if it harshly criticized the ways that the Ottomans were running Egypt. The two main national figures in Egypt in the early 1900s, Mostafa Kamil Pasha and Mohamed Fareed Pasha, were not only calling for independence from Britain, but also for the strengthening of ties with the Ottoman state and the global union of Muslims.[13] It is little surprise, then, that Fareed's most famous work was a volume on the history of the Ottoman Caliphate that was full of praise for the sultans, past and present.[14]

The defeat of the Ottomans in World War I and the subsequent dissolution of their empire in 1922–24, however, led to anger among Egyptian intellectuals, politicians, and thought leaders. Some of these leaders called on the Egyptian people to reject all kinds of regional pacts or unions inspired by Ottoman tradition and to adopt the standards of British and Western government; some even called for using Latin letters in writing Egyptian Arabic, inspired by Mostafa Kemal's Latinization of Turkish in 1928. These calls had been common among Egypt's liberals for some time, but gained more support following the end of the war.

Banna founded the Muslim Brotherhood in March 1928 in the context of this rhetoric. Banna's movement was a way of responding to one of the outcomes of World War I—defeat not of the Ottomans, per se, but rather the defeat of Egyptian intellectuals and politicians, who had adopted Western ways of thinking, ideologies, and lifestyle. This defeat had been evident in their political discourse decades earlier.

Banna's Muslim Brotherhood started off as a religious movement focusing mainly on moral advancement of Muslims in Egypt. But Banna also had politics in mind. Although the movement did not announce clear political stances until the 1930s, it began, early on, engaging with politics generally by advocating for political reform and national independence, without engaging in day-to-day party politics.

Banna moved to the capital in 1932 and established the Muslim Brotherhood's headquarters in downtown Cairo. In the same year, he created the Muslim Sisterhood to spread the call among Egyptian women. Later, during times of persecution, the role of the Sisters Department became more important when Brothers were arrested and Sisters became the fundraisers, breadwinners, and messengers between prison and the outside world. However, the women in the Muslim Brotherhood were never represented in the top executive committees or the legislative council (the Shura Council), nor did they even take part in institutional decision-making mechanisms. Ironically, the Muslim Sisterhood is a department that has been run by male supervisors since its inception ninety years ago.

The movement quickly opened its Students Department. The Muslim Brotherhood opened its first branches abroad in 1933 in Djibouti, and then other regional branches were opened in Morocco, Tunisia, Libya, Sudan, and several other countries.[15] These branches of the Brotherhood adopted similar structure, ideology, and methods to the Egyptian Brotherhood, but focused on local, domestic politics. In 1933, Banna held the second public conference for the Muslim Brotherhood; at the conference, the group started fundraising from members to establish economic enterprises and a publishing house.[16] The movement was gaining momentum among Egyptians, and in 1938 it issued *Al-Natheer*, the weekly magazine in which Banna announced the Brotherhood's "new step": to engage in party politics and to "reject [all] parties that do not agree with the [Brotherhood's] understanding of Islam."[17] In an editorial in the first issue of *Al-Natheer*, Banna stressed that turning to direct political work did not mean that the Brotherhood was contradicting its previous beliefs, but that a new phase had arrived for the work of the movement.[18]

Ambiguous Identity

In January 1939, Banna held the Brotherhood's Fifth Conference, which was arguably the most important public conference in the movement's history because he announced the main political framework of the Muslim Brotherhood. Since its inception, that framework has been catchy and powerful, but also idealistic, simplistic, and to some extent paradoxical even to the movement's devout followers. For example, in relation to the use of force and revolution, on the one hand, Banna said that the Brotherhood believed that the "constitutional system of government is the closest existing governing system in the entire world to Islam," and that it was not ready to "replace it with any other system." Banna also stressed that his movement "does not think about a revolution, does not rely on it, and does not trust its benefits and results." In the same breath, however, Banna said that the Muslim Brotherhood would "use practical force if there is no other feasible way" to achieve the group's ultimate goals, and that, when the Brothers use force, "they will be honest and noble, and will warn [their enemies] first … and will be satisfied to bear the consequences of their position."[19]

The Brotherhood's official interpretation of Banna's phrasing is that it was bounded by the context of the British occupation in Egypt at the time and that the Brotherhood would never use force against its own citizens or presiding governments. However, this ambiguity in its core positions led the Brotherhood leadership, at different moments in the organization's history—including the aftermath of the military coup of 2013—to split over the use of force against the regime, with each side citing Banna to support their stances.

In his letter to the Fifth Conference, Banna defined the Muslim Brotherhood as "a Salafi call, a Sunni way, a Sufi truth, a political organization, an athletic group, an intellectual and scientific association, an economic company, and a social idea."[20] With this multifaceted characterization of the movement, Banna sought to portray the Brotherhood as an inclusive movement capable of achieving different goals through a "one-size-fits-all" approach.[21] This allowed the movement to attract the support of people from very different social and religious backgrounds. However, in the absence of a charismatic leader and a clear ideology that could unify members, the organization was to face several internal crises and shocks over its identity.

During the 1939 conference, Banna summarized the ultimate goal of the Muslim Brotherhood: "to create a new generation of Muslims who can reformulate the Islamic ummah in all aspects of life."[22] In later letters, he repeated this broad aim, articulating seven stages of personal work through which Brothers would achieve it: (1) reform oneself to be a good Muslim, (2) establish a Muslim family, (3) guide (advise) society, (4) liberate the homeland from foreign powers, (5) reform the government to be Islamic, (6) restore the international entity of the Islamic ummah (a caliphate or a similar union), and (7) work to achieve the professorship (*ustadhiyya*, meaning to take on the role of a teacher) of the world by preaching the call of Islam.[23]

In 1941, Banna held the Brotherhood's sixth and final public conference at which he emphasized the Brotherhood's belief in "constitutional struggle" to achieve the movement's goals.[24] With World War II raging, Banna called on Britain to grant Egypt and Sudan their independence, and to pledge that British troops would remain stationed in Egypt only during the war. Banna did not support the British occupation of Egypt at any moment, but he was sensitive to the exigencies of the global conflict. Somewhat naively, Banna also used his letter to call on world leaders to view Islam as a possible solution for the salvation of the world during these turbulent times. Much of Banna's letter was full of political declarations and statistics about the Egyptian economic and social situation in the early 1940s; to the extent that he offered solutions for the country's problems, they were, again, simplistic, broad, and idealistic.

The Structure of the Muslim Brotherhood

In the years that followed, the movement's structure became more complicated and organized. The membership of the Muslim Brotherhood became a structured process that took years of spiritual socialization, ideological indoctrination, and, more importantly, organizational progression. Banna designed five tiers of membership for his followers:[25]

1. A potential recruit was a Sympathizer (*muhib*)
2. A neophyte recruit was a Supporter (*mu'ayyid*)
3. The next level of membership was an Associate (*muntasib*)
4. The next level was Organizer (*muntazim*)
5. A full member was an Active Brother (*akh a'amel*).

To move up from one tier to another, a member had to go through rigorous religious, social, and organizational training. This process took years and was under the supervision of the Upbringing Committee, the most powerful department in the organization.

Each Muslim Brotherhood member must participate, along with a number of their peers in the geographical area where they live, in a weekly pedagogical convening called an usra (family) meeting. Each family consists of five or more members, and has a mentor who is usually more senior than the others. Several families in a specific area constitute a branch, or *shu'ba*. Every branch has a shura council, a consultative council, and a captain that the branch's eligible members elect from those members above the Associate level. The unit above the branch is the region (*mantiqa*), which also has an elected shura council and a head, who must be an Active Brother. Above that, the regions in a specific governorate constitute an administrative office that runs the Brotherhood's business in the governorates and has its own shura council and president. A group of provinces constitute a sector (*qita'*), which helps facilitate communications between the leadership with the minimum number of leaders attending family meetings during crackdowns. The shura councils of the governorates elect the General Shura Council for the whole organization in Egypt. The Guidance Bureau members are chosen from the General Shura Council's members; the bureau in turn chooses the general guide of the Brotherhood.

The general guide usually appoints one or more deputies and a secretary-general who becomes responsible for managing what the Brotherhood calls central technical committees. These committees serve as internal departments in which every Brotherhood member usually volunteers. Before the military coup of 2013, the Brotherhood had twelve central technical committees, which included the Upbringing Committee, the Workers Committee, the Students Committee, the Professionals Committee, the Piety Committee, the Spreading of the Da'wa (the Islamic call) Committee, the Sisters Committee, the Media Committee, the Political Committee, and several others. These committees are represented at every organizational level, from the branch upward. The Guidance Bureau appoints heads of these committees, many of whom are usually selected from the bureau members themselves.

It is noteworthy that the women in the Muslim Brotherhood do not get to participate in most aspects of this structure. The Sisters have only two membership levels, which do not allow them to have voting powers, participate in internal elections, or take part in the decision-making process.

The complex organization that Banna designed proved powerful. However, it quickly became too big to control.

The Foundation of the Special Apparatus

In the early 1940s, Hassan al-Banna established a militant arm for the Muslim Brotherhood to participate in "guerilla actions inside and outside [Egypt], whether in resisting the British occupation, and the governments that support it, or [against the occupation] in Palestine."[26] The division—later known as the Special Apparatus—included mainly civilian members and later military members under the leadership of civilian Brotherhood members. Ironically, important recruits in the Special Apparatus included the young officer Gamal Abdel Nasser, as well as many members of what became the Apparatus of the Free Officers within the military and which staged the coup of 1952, founding the republic in Egypt.[27]

Along with the Special Apparatus, Banna established another department to recruit police officers and military men under the supervision of police officer Salah Shadi in 1944–45.[28] This department, named the Department of Units, aimed to spread the call of the Muslim Brotherhood among police officers and military officers. While the Special Apparatus was a secret regime inside the organization that no ordinary member would join or even know about, the Department of Units was like any other department within the Muslim Brotherhood. The Department of Units held public conferences and graduation ceremonies for police officers in the movement's headquarters with the attendance of high-ranking officers, senior university professors, and cabinet ministers.[29]

Between 1945 and 1948, the Special Apparatus recruited hundreds of members, established an internal intelligence unit, and gained power and legitimacy within the Muslim Brotherhood.[30] The activities of the apparatus ranged from surveilling government officials and infiltrating Egyptian political parties to attacking foreign businesses and British troops in Egypt. For the most part, and for technical and security reasons, the Special Apparatus enjoyed its status as an autonomous entity without close supervision from Banna or other leaders of the Brotherhood.[31] This autonomy led the apparatus's leadership to take decisions that were against Banna's will and beliefs. In March 1948, two members of the Special Apparatus assassinated Ahmed al-Khazendar, the president of the Cairo's Court of Appeal. There was a wave of condemnation, including from Banna himself, who was not consulted before the assassination.[32] In the months that followed, Special Apparatus members participated in the Palestine War of 1948 (also known as Israel's War of Independence) with more than 10,000 volunteers; the Muslim Brotherhood continues to take pride in this mobilization today. In Egypt, the apparatus's members attacked Jews and Jewish-owned businesses on the basis that their owners had links with the newly founded Jewish state in Palestine.

In December 1948, the Egyptian premier, Mahmoud Fahmy al-Nokrashy Pasha, issued a decree to dissolve the Muslim Brotherhood based on "the movement's attempts to overthrow the existing government." At the time, the Muslim Brotherhood was a major organization with hundreds of thousands of members and more than 2,000 branches all over Egypt, along with a regional presence in several countries in the Middle East and Africa. Following the decision, the government arrested many Muslim Brotherhood members and leaders, affecting Banna's ability to connect with members of his own organization.

The End of Hassan al-Banna's Movement

On December 28, 1948, just days after Nokrashy issued his decree, he was assassinated by a member of the Special Apparatus. In January 1949, Banna issued a furious statement condemning the assassination, in which he said "They are not Brotherhood [members], and not even Muslims."[33] But Banna himself was shot in downtown Cairo less than a month later and died on February 12, 1949; it has never been confirmed who was responsible for the assassination. Following Banna's death, the Muslim Brotherhood faced an organizational power struggle that could not be solved internally. To end the conflict, the group's leaders, after two years of internal struggle, deferred to the leadership of Hassan al-Hudaybi, a respected judge who was not an official member of the Muslim Brotherhood, despite being one of Banna's close confidants.

Under Hudaybi, the Muslim Brotherhood went through a series of crises that brought an end to the movement as Banna had founded it. The movement was now divided between different leaders, and the Special Apparatus was growing more powerful as chaos consumed Egypt.

Despite Banna's teachings rejecting revolution as a principle, the Brotherhood fully supported the 1952 coup that ended the monarchy. The deeply corrupt monarchy was neither willing nor able to achieve national independence, especially after its suppression of national forces and parties and Egypt's humiliating defeat in Palestine.

In the following two years, Egypt's new government turned on the Brotherhood, despite the fact that the organization had supported its rise to power. Taking advantage of the Brotherhood's internal conflicts and its lack of a political project, the government waged a relentless war to uproot the organization. One of the main reasons for this animosity was the Muslim Brotherhood's support for Mohamed Naguib, the first president the junta appointed after the coup. Naguib sought to establish a democracy in Egypt and to oversee the return of the officers to their barracks. Nasser, however, was pursuing full and uncontested power.

In the spring of 1954, the Muslim Brotherhood led mass protests to demand the establishment of democracy in Egypt, and many members and leaders were arrested in the following weeks. In October 1954, Mahmoud Abdel Latif, a member of the Special Apparatus, fired eight shots at Gamal Abdel Nasser while the leader was speaking at a public event in Alexandria, but failed to hit him. Abdel Latif was arrested on the spot, and in the following days the authorities arrested more than 24,000 members of the Brotherhood, according to the group's estimates, including its general guide, Hudaybi. Nasser held military trials for the Brotherhood. These trials led to the execution of six Brotherhood leaders, among whom were four leaders of the Special Apparatus.[34]

The Brotherhood never officially adhered to the regime's narrative of the assassination attempt, insisting that it was a "farce" designed by Nasser and his security apparatus to entrap the Muslim Brotherhood.[35] Some Brotherhood leaders believe that the Special

Apparatus acted independently without the knowledge of Hudaybi, and that the government knew about the assassination plan beforehand and allowed it to happen in a controlled setting to entrap the movement.[36]

Following the arrest of Hudaybi, the Muslim Brotherhood groups in the Arab countries formed an executive office led by Mostafa al-Sibai who had founded the Syrian Muslim Brotherhood in 1942 after meeting with Banna during his studies in Egypt in the 1930s.[37] At the time, the Muslim Brotherhood had already established branches in most Arab countries, including Jordan (1945), Sudan (1945), Palestine (1946), Kuwait (1947), Iraq (1949), Libya (late 1940s), Lebanon (early 1950s), and Algeria (1953).[38] The international organization of the Muslim Brotherhood had been growing ever since. These international branches of the Brotherhood, as noted above, applied the Brotherhood's philosophy to domestic issues in their respective countries, but also formed an international network that provided a kind of organizational safety net in times of crisis, such as Nasser's crackdown.

The Sayyid Qutb Effect

Shortly before the attempted assassination of Nasser, the Muslim Brotherhood recruited a writer who would soon become the most influential intellectual in the history of the Muslim Brotherhood: Sayyid Qutb. An established literary critic, Qutb joined the movement in late 1953, and quickly became the head of one of its departments and the chief editor of the Brotherhood's weekly magazine.[39] In the 1954 trials, Qutb was sentenced to fifteen years in jail, most of which he spent in hospital before he was released for medical reasons in May 1964.[40] In 1965, a group of young Muslim Brotherhood members who had been working for several years on forming a unit within the movement to revive the Muslim Brotherhood after the crisis of 1954 asked Qutb to join them and be their guide.[41] The unit already had Hudaybi's approval to study the Quran and Islam, but its members were planning the assassination of Nasser and exploring plans to overthrow the regime through a series of attacks.[42]

Hudaybi, who was under house arrest at the time, could not control the movement, and the young zealots were taking the lead. In August 1965, the regime discovered the unit and initiated a new wave of arrests of tens of thousands of Muslim Brotherhood members, including Qutb and his sister, and Hudaybi and six of his family members.[43] After a public trial, the court sentenced Qutb and two other leaders to death. During the year in jail that preceded his execution, Qutb produced *Milestones*, a book that would come to be considered among the most influential literary pieces for many Islamic movements, particularly Salafi jihadist groups.

Qutb's *Milestones* took on a life of its own. There were differing perceptions among Muslim Brotherhood members. While many members and leaders (including the general guides Mohammed Hamed Abulnasr [in office 1986–96], Mostafa Mashour [in office 1996–2002], Mohammed Mahdi Akef [in office 2004–10], and Mohammed Badie [in office since 2010]) felt that the book did not call for violence and did not constitute a departure from Hassan al-Banna's peaceful call, others saw Qutb's ideas as alienating to most Muslims and Muslim communities. Among the leaders who rejected Qutb's thought were Hudaybi himself; his son, Ma'mun al-Hudaybi (the Brotherhood's sixth general guide, 2002–4); Fareed Abdelkhaleq, Banna's close associate and former member of the Guidance Bureau; and Yusuf al-Qaradawi, one of the most influential contemporary Muslim scholars worldwide and formerly a leading figure in the Brotherhood, before leaving the organization. These differences in how figures in the Muslim Brotherhood viewed Qutb led to major conflicts among leaders regarding how to respond to the violent crackdown in the post-Morsi era.

The Brotherhood never officially criticized Qutb's book, although it did not accept it as widely as some might assume. The Brotherhood responded to *Milestones'* widespread popularity by noting that it called for a level of alienation from society and even for denouncing people's religious practices (*takfir*). The Brotherhood then released *Dua'at la Qudat* (*Preachers, Not Judges*), a seminal Brotherhood book that emphasized that the organization's role was to proselytize, and not to judge or exclude anyone from the Islamic faith. Shortly before his death, Ma'mun al-Hudaybi got angry at his grandson for reading *Milestones,* telling him that "it does not represent the Muslim Brotherhood's ideas, and that Qutb's ideas do not represent the Brotherhood."[44] The point is that Qutb's ideas never represented the organization, even though they resonated with some members at one point in time. However, the 1965 generation—of which Qutb was a part—lived through the experience of jail, torture, and executions, and have remained influential and vital to the organization's trajectory. Mohammed Badie, Mahmoud Ezzat, and Ibrahim Munir, the current highest-ranking officials (the latter until his death in November 2022), all belong to this generation and all had firsthand encounters with Qutb.

The Second Reconstitution

Despite his best efforts, Nasser was not able to eradicate the Muslim Brotherhood. During the 1950s and 1960s, the core members of the Brotherhood were still active though at a lower capacity. As one leader of the 1965 organization put it, "The leadership decided to have a system without an organization."[45] The Brothers simply tried to maintain their relations and support each other without having a hierarchical organization. This strategy was efficient in securing the safety of tens of thousands of Muslim Brotherhood members who maintained their beliefs and affiliation without announcing them to the public. However, the defeat of the Egyptian army in the 1967 Arab–Israeli War allowed for the rise of religious sentiment among the general public, which opened the door for the Muslim Brotherhood to rebuild its organization. Taking advantage of the relative political openness during Sadat's regime (1970–81), Umar al-Tilmisani led the organization through its second reconstitution and expanded its presence in universities and professional syndicates. Throughout this period, the Muslim Brotherhood built not only on religious sentiment but on the failure of the state to represent most Egyptians.[46]

Active students gained civic and political skills that set them up for a life of political activism within the confines of an authoritarian state. During the same period, as the political situation grew more tolerant of the Brotherhood, members who had fled Egypt under Nasser started returning. These returnees came with the experiences of having started Islamic organizations in a wide array of countries around the world. The second reconstitution opened the doors for the organization to rebuild itself throughout the 1980s and 1990s. Many of these institutions and bylaws were not drafted in documents seen as foundational, but rather aimed to ensure a sense of continuity and legitimize ongoing processes and precedent. While many of the institutions and processes this generation built contributed to the organization's longevity, the organization failed to build rigorous accountability mechanisms to address grievances among members.[47] This absence of conflict-resolution mechanisms within the Brotherhood was the direct reason for several crises that the movement has experienced since the 1990s.

Many Muslim Brotherhood members who left Egypt during the 1960s (fleeing persecution under Nasser) and in the 1970s (seeking better life opportunities in the Gulf states, including Saudi Arabia, the United Arab Emirates, Kuwait, and Qatar) returned to Egypt with more organizational experience and financial resources. Influenced by the conservative Salafi version of Islam, which is dominant in the Gulf, some of these returnees effectively influenced the Egyptian movement with relatively more conservative ideas around women, Islamic governance, and democracy. Partly as a result, in the 1990s the Muslim Brotherhood reopened discussions around the hijab, democracy, and political participation—issues that were settled during Banna's time. In the 1980s, the Brotherhood had been keen to build electoral and political coalitions with both liberal and leftist parties. But that began to change, and by the time of the 2011 revolution, the Salafi effect on the Brotherhood was pronounced. After the revolution, the Brotherhood shortsightedly formed coalitions with the Salafi parties based on identity politics and religious affiliations in the several elections in which they took part.

With the return of many Brotherhood members to Egypt, the organization started, in the mid- and late 1980s, to focus much of its work on building institutions and entities within society, such as schools, health centers, charity associations, and mosques. At the same time, the group participated heavily in professional syndicates and labor unions, such as the Lawyers Syndicate, Doctors Syndicate, and Engineers Syndicate. As we show in Chapter 1 of this book, this expertise reintroduced the Muslim Brotherhood and its members to Egyptian society as organized, well-intentioned, and straightforward, which helped the movement when the time came for free public elections.

But while many exiled Brotherhood members had returned, many others remained abroad. In the mid-1980s, Egyptian Brotherhood members who had fled the country established an association to coordinate the efforts of the group's sizable diaspora, which is distinct from the fellowships of Brotherhood offshoots in other countries. In Chapter 2 of this book, we delve into detail about the presence of Egyptian Brotherhood members abroad.

The Brotherhood grew increasingly open to public-facing work and to politics. It ran for elections in the 1980s (in coalition with the movement's historical rival, the liberal Wafd Party), and in the 1990s (in coalition with the leftist Egyptian Labour Party in 1990). The security crackdown and the military trials of Muslim Brotherhood leaders in 1995 compromised the project significantly, however. Security forces detained senior leaders and tried them in military courts again, in 2000. Many were detained for years on end on trumped up charges. The organization retreated.

It was also in the 1990s that the Brotherhood made relatively more progressive proposals regarding democracy and democratic participation, women's role in the public sphere, and Coptic Christians, especially vis-à-vis the permissibility of holding the presidency. On the latter point, the Brotherhood took an official position of no position—an attempt to avoid taking a side in competing schools of Islamic jurisprudence on the matter, and leaving the decision about whether a Copt could be president "to the people."[48] These positions may not seem progressive, but they were also not radical or exclusionary. More importantly, they emphasize a blurry line between the organization and the larger Egyptian population where ideas about religiosity and religious performance are always in flux.

The 1980s and 1990s offered a peculiar challenge for the organization in terms of navigating the lines between the religious and the political and between the public and the private, and in terms of the identity of the organization itself. Moments in which the Brotherhood opened up to political engagement and participation were often followed by moments of immense crackdowns with inexplicable violence, torture, killings, and loss. The Brotherhood's shape, strategies, and policies were never fixed. They are all the outcome of the experiences of the different generations it has comprised—generations who endured immense state violence, reacted to that violence differently, and made different decisions about how to pass the organization on to subsequent generations. The shape, strategies, and policies are the legacy of authoritarianism, not religious politics.

In some ways, the Brotherhood never recovered from the crises of legitimacy and identity that followed Banna's assassination. Banna did not leave behind detailed instructions—only general guideposts—and no general guide has had comparable charisma to fill the void. Successive generations interpreted these guideposts differently.

At times, the plurality this created within the organization contributed to its longevity. But it also meant that, at any given moment, the organization included people who had very different views on crucial issues including violence, political participation, or even the permissibility of certain acts, such as listening to music, watching movies, participating in Sufi ceremonies, women foregoing the *niqab* (face veil), and men not growing beards.

Further, this legacy meant that the Brotherhood was shaped more by repression and resilience than it was by ideology. And in this context, the Brotherhood prized secrecy, loyalty, and trust over openness or competency—even when it used nominally democratic mechanisms, such as the Shura Council.

This book posits that the Brotherhood today faces three main crises: a crisis of identity, a crisis of legitimacy, and a crisis of membership. Nearly a decade since the 2013 coup that overthrew Mohamed Morsi, claimed the lives of thousands, and detained tens of thousands, the organization continues to be torn between dead ends in Egyptian politics and complex crises within its ranks. These crises animate the organization's work. But unless they are resolved, they may threaten the longevity and efficacy of the organization. This is the most existential threat that the Brotherhood has faced to date, and so long as the third reconstitution currently underway fails to address some of these issues, the organization may be doomed to disarray.

Methodology

Before delving into how we came to put this project together, it is important to define what it is and what it is not. This is a book about the Muslim Brotherhood from 2013 to 2022. It is written with a policy audience in mind. While we hope it can have broader appeal, choosing this audience gave us the liberty to step beyond the confines of academic research and situate our work in contemporary events—and not necessarily within theoretical discussions on social movements, Islamist politics, the diaspora organizations, or even state violence. The research for the book was conducted with an ethnographic sensibility. To that end, this project is heavily based on interviews the authors conducted with current and former members of the Muslim Brotherhood. These interviews took place across five countries and four continents in our attempt to cover the breadth of the changes and developments the organization has undergone since 2013. Primarily for security reasons, this project did not include interviews with members based in Egypt. Whether remotely or in person, the interviews were conducted using trauma-informed approaches, as many of those we interviewed are former detainees and asylees.

The gender breakdown of the interviewees skewed heavily toward men, as the researchers had difficulty gaining access to women members. We acknowledge that this does not accurately reflect the reality of the role of the Sisterhood in the organization. We consulted an array of secondary literature, primarily ethnographic, focused on Brotherhood members' lived experiences. We also recognize that women are not represented in the structure of the Brotherhood or in leadership positions—an issue that will be discussed further in the coming pages.

Many interviewees' names were changed to pseudonyms; the reader can easily identify such pseudonyms in the book because we have only given such interviewees first names. We did this to maintain the safety of the interviewees, as the rise of transnational repression has put at risk the security of dissidents and researchers alike. Some minor details were also altered to disguise identities.

Recruitment for these interviews relied, initially, on personal networks and subsequently on snowball sampling. This method was unavoidable for many reasons. First, the subject matter is sensitive and, for many members, secretive. The organization contends with the reality of being designated a terrorist organization in many countries and the looming threat of designation in others, including the United States.

Second, the questions related to command and control came at a time in the organization's history when it was undergoing a vertical split. Many of the processes, committees, and high-level officials that played consequential roles between 2013 and early 2022 were ousted, as we discuss below. Finally, the organization occupies a precarious space as a publicly very private organization—the organization is at once politically engaged and appeals to a broad base, but continues to maintain secretive processes and leaders. An organization that defines itself as secretive while millions of members associate with it, to varying degrees of publicity, is a paradox that we had to navigate during our discussions, interviews, and networking. Practically, this meant that the process of building trust with interviewees often took incredible effort and tremendous amounts of time. A number of interviews were conducted over two or more sessions. Further, unless interviewees vouched for us, some of the interviews would not have taken place. Even after reaching out to them through trusted contacts, several key Brotherhood members and leaders refused to talk to us, often due to fear of the authorities' retaliation against their family members still in Egypt, while some refused because they simply couldn't trust us.

Of note in considering our descriptions of interviewees: Membership in the Brotherhood can be an elusive concept. There are tiers of membership that reflect the level of responsibilities members have taken on. Moving from one tier to another often involved a transition period in which members engaged with different curricula, taking what is called a "promotion course" in which they studied specific aspects of the Brotherhood's ideology or tactics. Only then, if their superiors approved, were they promoted. These courses continued in prison and throughout the first few years after 2013. In exile, some of these tiers of memberships took on different meanings. Some people left the official ranks of the Brotherhood because they felt as though the current organization did not resemble the one they joined in Egypt. Others were demoted in their ranks in what they described as punishment for public political stances they had taken. Finally, the organization has left thousands with a feeling of being unrepresented, so that, while they never officially left, their membership fizzled out.

It is important to note that this project also relied on documents that the Brotherhood either officially produced for internal or external audiences and others that some factions endorsed in the aftermath of the 2013 massacre. Such documents include at least one that was produced in prison. These documents, and how and why they were disseminated, give us an insight into how the organization thinks of its audiences and how it positions itself at different junctures.

PART II
The Brotherhood's Three Crises

1
The Identity Crisis

"This is not our revolution."
 —A member of the Muslim Brotherhood's Guidance Bureau, 2011[1]

An Organization for What? An Organization for Whom?

The failure of the Muslim Brotherhood's experiment with power continues to be the subject of fierce debates, especially given it was long assumed that the Brotherhood would be the natural victor of any regime change in Cairo after Hosni Mubarak. This chapter aims to explain the failure of the Brotherhood, and argues that it had its roots in the organization's tactical responses to authoritarian and competitive pressures, which were well suited for allowing it to survive Mubarak's authoritarianism, but reduced its ability to cope with the political landscape after the 2011 uprising. We argue that the Brotherhood's political failure was neither predetermined nor driven by ideological reasons—contrary to essentialist analyses that assume an inherent tension between the tenets of religious movements and their desire to seek office in modern states.[2] There were also pressures on the organization from below, given the so-called Islamic resurgence (*al-sahwa al-islamiyya*) and rival Islamic discourses that broke the Brotherhood's hegemony on nonviolent Islamism. A more modernized Islamic public sphere from the late 1990s onward started stirring debates on complex social and political issues, most importantly through the expansion of Internet usage and the emergence of a new religious intelligentsia, which exposed the rather petty and populist ideas shaping the Brotherhood narrative among the educated middle classes. More pressing for the organization, however, was Salafism, with which it had to deal to avoid losing ground among the lower classes, who outnumber the middle classes in a lower-middle-income country.[3] The ways in which these elements and their historical precedents have animated the organization's perception of itself and its role, and how they manifested in our period of study, constitutes what we term an identity crisis.

Throughout the twentieth century, Egypt's largest independent political organization responded to vertical authoritarian pressures from the regime and horizontal ontological pressures from "fellow Brothers" with short-term tactics for survival that solidified its traditional strongholds and maintained the grip of its leadership on its rank and file. Yet, those same tactics diluted the political tradition of the Brotherhood, diminished its ability to grapple with social changes in Egypt before 2011, and undermined its capacity to behave as a national political actor after the uprising. Further, they transformed the Brotherhood into a mere reservoir of religious votes, relatively ineffective at influencing national politics despite the sheer quantity of its members.

The January 2011 uprising came as a surprise to most politicians at home, as well as commentators both home and abroad, and was no less surprising for the Brotherhood. The organization had just put its house in order by cementing its internal status quo throughout 2005–10, and had chosen an archconservative as supreme leader in 2010. The speed of the events of the uprising forced the Brotherhood to chart a new political course under the stress of rising expectations, mutual mistrust with many state agencies, and inter-Islamist competition. The organization coped with these conflicting sources of pressure by pursuing day-to-day tactics in the spirit of the pre-2011 era. Although these tactics kept the Brotherhood alive, they fell short of enabling it to propose a convincing political project, communicate effectively to the vibrant and multifaceted post-2011 public sphere, or form a solid national front to enhance its negotiating position with the military.

In the aftermath of the uprising, the governing Supreme Council of the Armed Forces (SCAF) appeared to quickly reach a consensus with the Brotherhood to contain the volatility of the streets, and soon formed a committee for drafting amendments to the 1971 constitution. Most non-Islamist 2011 revolutionaries saw the constitution as basically unamendable—it was a relic of the ancien régime that had to be abolished altogether if political parties were serious about enshrining a new state based on the legitimacy of the revolution.[4]

The Islamic movements, for their part, had pragmatic reasons for desiring a return to normalcy, which would be achieved faster with an amended constitution than with a new one written from scratch. The Muslim Brotherhood, which had suffered the brunt of Egypt's last period of absolute rule under Gamal Abdel Nasser, was obsessed with the heightened possibility of another episode of such arbitrary rule emanating from the institutional fluidity brought about by the 2011 revolution. Nasser's regime was not the only period it had been subjected to arbitrary power: Egypt, despite a long constitutional and legal tradition, has a longer and more entrenched tradition of arbitrary rule in which authoritarians, at several instances, legitimized themselves on the grounds that they were protecting a revolution or providing swift modernization.

In contrast, the 1971 constitution, drafted upon Anwar Sadat's arrival to power, had come to embody the end of Nasser's "revolutionary legitimacy" and the return to "constitutional legitimacy."[5] This transformation allowed the regime to create a new breed of conservative political and legal intelligentsia, and ushered in an era in which populist one-man rule diminished. For the Brotherhood, this constitution guaranteed a bare minimum of consensual politics—it was a sort of bird in hand, while a new, theoretically more perfect constitution represented two in the bush.

SCAF, the Brotherhood, and the voters all wanted an end to the short uprising for divergent reasons. It was only with the electoral contests for parliament and presidential office that it became apparent that there were contradictions within this seemingly coherent bloc. Later, it would become clear that the Brotherhood's grip on an overwhelmingly religious society was not as strong as had been supposed; that there were cracks in the social coalition that staged the uprising; and that a counterrevolutionary force was buying time to put its house in order.

The Origins of Islamic Fraternity

Politics as a modern practice developed in Egypt in the aftermath of the 1919 revolution and the foundation of the Wafd Party. Social and economic shifts during World War I constituted a point of no return for the relations between the masses and the rising nationalist elite on one hand, and the one-man rule of the royal palace and the colonial administration of the British on the other. Throughout the ups and downs of Egypt's three-decade experiment with partial parliamentary democracy, university campuses came to play a crucial role, providing an alternative conduit for politics when the democratic process was strangled by the palace, especially for a new generation of a gradually expanding middle class after World War II. The Free Officers' power grab in 1952, which dissolved political parties and suspended democratic politics for almost six decades, sealed the fate of universities as a central ground for politics and protest, and a cocoon for molding successive generations of Egyptian politicians and activists. Although Nasser's Arab nationalist regime commanded the streets with minimal opposition for almost fifteen years, its defeat in the 1967 Arab-Israeli War unleashed student protests in 1968, and university politics made a forceful return after a decade of unprecedented authoritarianism.

Egypt's first university, Cairo University, was founded in 1908. A decade later, the campus was a staging ground for the 1919 wave of nationalist mobilization. In the 1930s, it was Cairo University students who spearheaded the 1935 uprising against British occupation, leading to the conclusion of the 1936 Anglo-Egyptian Treaty formally bringing the occupation to an end. The 1930s saw the emergence of radical ideological movements that gradually broke away from the Wafd Party's constitutional conservatism. These ranged from the rightist Young Egypt Party to several communist movements. Alexandria University, was founded in 1938 in Egypt's second most populous city, and enrollment gradually increased in both universities. In this atmosphere of radical politics, with expanding higher education and—consequently—modern middle-class professions, the Brotherhood rose to occupy a firm place in Egyptian politics and society under the leadership of its founder, Hassan al-Banna.[6]

Banna was popular among the petty bourgeoisie that had only recently urbanized, with many having received a traditional Arab-Islamic education in *katatib* (traditional Islamic primary schools, singular *kuttab*), before making the transition to a modern high school and then to a university—as Banna himself did. The mix between modern and urban aspirations, nationalist sentiments, and conservative religious backgrounds came to define the Brotherhood's rank and file for decades to come. As the organization mushroomed and opened branches across Egypt, its evolution was intertwined with that of the wider society, probably more than any other institution in the country, aside from the state itself.

Egypt witnessed a continuous rise in university enrollment, with the absolute number of university students increasing tenfold between 1930 and 1952. Between 1955 and 1965, the university student population almost doubled, in tandem with a decision by the Nasser government to make university education free for all. Al-Azhar, an Islamic institute of higher learning founded in the tenth century, was designated a national university in 1961, forfeiting its independence and significantly increasing its student population; it opened science and humanities departments like any other university.[7]

The following decades brought various transformations for Egypt, and the position of the middle class became more complex. Nasser died in 1970, closing the first postcolonial chapter of Egypt's history. Egypt's military performed effectively in the October 1973 war with Israel, boosting Sadat's profile, and easing the way for him to open to the West, make peace with Israel, and transform the country into a capitalist economy. But as the Egyptian state disavowed some of its earlier socioeconomic commitments and nationalist policies after Nasser, its capacity for commanding the masses diminished. As a result, the state started to accept the inevitability of a partial political opening, allowing the Brotherhood to gradually reemerge onto the political scene. Sadat was eager to defeat the Nasserists and communists who staunchly protested his policies, and he thought of a cautious opening to the Brotherhood as a counterbalance to the entrenched influence of Nasserists, especially in Egypt's universities, which were now teeming with an unprecedented number of students and a wave of political activism.

Shaken by student uprisings in 1968 and 1972, enrollment in Egyptian universities was expanded to include all high school graduates. These expanded admissions were partly an effort to make the student population more diverse, with a supposedly more conservative and religious cohort from rural backgrounds.[8] Consequently, the university population nearly tripled between the mid-1970s and mid-1980s, and six universities were founded in the provinces, along with several branches of public universities in smaller towns.[9] With this boom came a new generation of Islamist activists who were, at first, on good terms with the Sadat regime.[10]

Brotherhood members who languished in prisons under Nasser's rule were released throughout the 1970s. Recent university graduates, in search of a more enduring political platform than campus activism, gravitated to the older generation of Islamists, and sought experience from veterans of the pre-1952 era. This intergenerational symbiosis between those who came of age in the 1970s, and older veterans released from prison in the same decade, had a lasting legacy in molding the so-called historical leadership of the Brotherhood.

The Brotherhood Bounces Back

Before Nasser's brutal campaign against the Brotherhood, the organization had nearly 70,000 members. By the mid-1970s, fewer than one hundred of those released from prison remained active as an organization to continue what Banna had begun.[11] The majority of these active members were former members of the Brotherhood's militant Special Apparatus—including Mahmoud Ezzat. Ezzat had renounced violence in 1969, but he and other ex-Special Apparatus men had internalized the Special Apparatus's secretive and Soviet-like ways of political organization. The Brotherhood was revived, but the "public activist" generation—those who were mostly former student activists—was deprived of effective political power, while the core of the Brotherhood came to be dominated by former Special Apparatus men, who eventually controlled the whole organization.

Al-Gama'a al-Islamiyya (the Islamic Group), a movement that swept Egyptian student politics in the early 1970s, split by the end of that decade, with most of its branches in Cairo and the Delta (northern Egypt) joining the Muslim Brotherhood under its new general guide, Umar al-Tilmisani, and its branches in most Upper Egyptian provinces establishing an eponymous organization (al-Gama'a al-Islamiyya), which chose to adopt violence against the regime. A smaller group in Alexandria established the "Salafi Call" network (*al-Da'wa al-Salafiyya*), and stayed largely aloof from politics and on good terms with security agencies throughout the Mubarak era. As for the Brotherhood, its second reconstitution under Tilmisani witnessed a resurrection of Banna's national conservatism and a renunciation of Qutbism.[12] The young student movement essentially became the forebearer of three Muslim religious groups—the militant al-Gama'a al-Islamiyya, the Salafi Call, and the resurgent

Muslim Brotherhood—that dominated Egypt's society for almost four decades albeit without any formal political authority.

In the first decade of Mubarak's presidency, the Brotherhood gradually grew in strength and appeal. Egypt was a nation in flux in the 1970s and 1980s, with hundreds of thousands demobilized after war, and hundreds of thousands graduating from universities in record numbers into a weak economy that was abandoning the urge for industrialization and rushing to partly dismantle Nasser's welfarism. The fragile state, which previously relied on Nasser's popular appeal to command the streets, found itself shaken by an unprecedented popular uprising in 1977 against reducing subsidies on basic commodities, and further shocked by Sadat's assassination in 1981. Mubarak's regime came to power seeking containment of new social groups, Islamist activists, and former Nasserist bureaucrats, rather than continuing Sadat's costly confrontation with the opposition, which had intensified toward the end of his presidency.

Mubarak was assisted in defusing social tension by a booming oil-based economy in Iraq and the Gulf, which offered millions of employment opportunities for Egypt's recent graduates. In addition, Tilmisani's national and nonviolent conservatism enjoyed the fruits of an entente with the Mubarak regime. Mubarak was focused on battling violent Islamism throughout the 1980s; during the same time, the Brotherhood expanded its social power across Egypt as a nonviolent Islamist group on good terms with the state. Partially free parliamentary elections were held twice, in 1984 and 1987, and the results made the Brotherhood's rising power evident on a national scale. In 1984, a resurrected Wafd Party garnered 56 percent of opposition votes after making an alliance with the Brotherhood, while the Socialist (later Islamist) Labour Party got only 26 percent. But in 1987, the Labour Party managed to win almost 56 percent of opposition votes after it struck an alliance with the Brotherhood, while the Wafd dropped to 36 percent.[13] A similar dominance took place in trade unions, where the Brotherhood managed to organize its members to control important syndicates and restructure them to provide modest benefits for their members.[14]

The rise of the Brotherhood was not just a matter of voting blocs and popular appeal. The organization also came to define a new class that arose from doing business in the post-Nasser era, as well as from making enormous savings working in the Gulf. By the late 1980s, eight out of the top eighteen business families in Egypt were associated with the Brotherhood. This new Islamic society, not exclusively under the command of the Brotherhood, but heavily under its influence, gradually mushroomed to dominate the public sphere, both socially and economically. The state slowly and uneasily coped, and its affiliated old middle class slightly gravitated toward the Islamists—at least culturally, with their lifestyles gradually conforming to the new social codes. Still, much of the old-guard middle class continued to mistrust the Brotherhood politically, convinced by the official state narrative that Islamist parties did not make for effective politicians, were simply hungry for power, and would destabilize Egypt and its relations with Western powers. This mistrust led to a dissonance between the increasing religiosity of middle-class Egyptians and their political affiliation—a dissonance whose resolution eluded the Brotherhood for years, and contributed to its downfall in 2013.

In the 1980s, Islamic ideas also became more influential in areas outside of politics. Islamist capital, for example, became a center of gravity in the economy. Islamic charity and solidarity programs also began to become a substitute for the disappearing welfare state. Islamic networks arose in most corners of lower and lower-middle class neighborhoods, most of which had been built hastily and illegally around the old city center to house millions of rural immigrants. Islamic networks also became dominant in most of the Delta governorates. They arose as well among the upper classes as mistrust of the state took hold, particularly with regard to official financial institutions. Islamic networks included private mosques (constituting more than 80 percent of mosques in Egypt by the late 1980s);

welfare voluntary organizations including clinics, schools and charity; and Islamic for-profit organizations including businesses, Islamic banks, commercial enterprises, and publishing houses.[15]

The Islamic resurgence, as it came to be called, meant that a large segment of the population was increasingly involved in modern associational life, even if this was on the basis of religious rather than nationalist mobilization. The Brotherhood's role in the syndicates was key, as it helped incorporate socially and economically new segments into the fold of welfarist institutions, in the process increasing the syndicates' revenues and their capacity for service provision.[16] The Brotherhood and other Islamists developed tactics to socially expand while deferring any overt political action. Meanwhile, the Mubarak regime's campaign against violent groups throughout the 1980s bred a robust security sector and a network of patronage that ensured that any form of Islamist social power did not translate into a political threat. The Brotherhood, who, of course, did not intend to only build social networks forever, began to harbor political ambitions, and started thinking of ways to acquire political power in a largely authoritarian system. In this they were inspired by the Sudanese experiment, which saw Sudan's Islamists gradually rise in power until they dominated the political system in 1989, to be later deposed in a coup led by Omar al-Bashir ten years later.[17]

The Mubarak regime was aware that the sprawling social networks of the Brotherhood and other Islamists constituted a threat. When the regime emerged stronger in the 1990s, it revoked the uneasy and tacit understanding it had with the Brotherhood. The regime had less need for partial political tolerance of the opposition, and it discovered a covert plan of the Brotherhood's for acquiring political power.

Where the State Fails, the Brotherhood Comes In

The 1990s in Egypt was the quintessential Mubarak decade. The fall of the Soviet Union, which emboldened many U.S. allies, reinforced

Mubarak's pro-Western foreign policy. This led to Egypt's participation in the 1990–91 Gulf War—its first military excursion since 1973. Significantly, Egypt also mediated peace talks between the Palestinians and Israel. Gone were the days of rebellious nationalist officers in the army's ranks, and the rather smooth participation of Egypt in a U.S.-led war against a fellow Arab army was a signal that Arab nationalism had been largely tamed within the military.

After its participation in the Gulf War, Egypt was granted substantial debt relief by the Paris Club, averting a fiscal crisis. This debt relief allowed Egypt to maintain heavy subsidies on basic commodities (including oil) while increasing spending on the security sector, giving the Mubarak regime a new lease on life. Meanwhile, the war against violent Islamism continued until 1998, when al-Gama'a al-Islamiyya finally laid down its arms. The regime then turned its attention to the Brotherhood, aiming to curtail its political gains.

The first blow to the Brotherhood came in 1992, when security forces stormed the offices of Salsabil, a computer company owned by prominent Brotherhood members Khairat al-Shater and Hassan Malek. In the raid, the security forces found draft plans for the Brotherhood's political "enablement" (*tamkin*). The plans allegedly included "classified military projects; disinformation activities with the media; and plans to falsify association elections."[18]

The regime began taking more assertive steps to block the Brotherhood's political ambitions. An associations law (Law 100) passed by parliament in 1993 required a 50 percent quorum of registered members in board elections, effectively hobbling the Brotherhood, because its successes relied on organizing supporters in generally low-voter-turnout syndicate elections. In 1993, the government placed the Syndicate of Engineers, which had a Brotherhood-dominated board of directors, under official custodianship and dissolved its board.

In 1994, an amendment to the Egyptian Universities Act undermined the Brotherhood's power in the governing councils of university faculty clubs, and abolished the election of faculty deans who would now be appointed by university presidents. The bar association faced a similar fate in 1995, followed by a wider crackdown that saw two trials of dozens of prominent Brotherhood members before a military court. Further amendments to the associations law in 1995 included judicial supervision of elections, which afforded the regime a new avenue to meddle with votes, through regime-friendly administrators appointed by judges.[19]

As hardline securitized policies gradually replaced the containment of the 1980s, the Brotherhood came under increasing pressure. During this period, in 1996, the Brotherhood's fourth general guide, Mohammed Hamed Abulnasr (whose tenure started in 1986), passed away, and was succeeded by the arch-conservative Mostafa Mashour.

At this time, the societal strata that had supported Nasser had shrunk, and there was no real non-Islamist opposition to speak of. The so-called secular intelligentsia had been gradually co-opted by the state in the face of resurgent Islamism, and was reduced to being a state-dependent actor that barely crossed "red lines," even if it voiced opposition to many of the state's post-Nasserist policies. Omar Hussein, a former Brotherhood student leader, confirmed that by the time his generation enrolled in universities (in the mid-1990s) it wasn't Islamists versus leftists, but rather Islamists versus security agents. "You were either an Islamist or an *amnagi* [security collaborator]," Hussein said.[20] Mubarak's regime, which, unlike Nasser's, did not espouse any clear political ideology, expanded its power by recruiting the secular intelligentsia into its expanding constellation of security institutions. Mubarak gained a significant advantage by luring many non-Islamists who feared the Brotherhood's growing power into allying with the regime. Despite its small number, this secular intelligentsia dominated the media and the cultural scene, two arenas from which Islamists were largely absent. This absence was partly a result of the state actually barring them from using national media outlets and cultural platforms to communicate with or influence society, but it was also partly a result of the limited tools and knowledge on the part of the Islamists. The Brotherhood's almost total absence from private media production before 2011, and its modest capacity at utilizing media through a few television stations in Istanbul after 2013, testifies to the latter point.[21]

The Mubarak regime was largely successful in excluding the Brotherhood from institutions that had been central to state power since independence, such as syndicates and university boards. Rather than contesting the regime in areas it dominated, the Brotherhood pivoted to expand where state reach was fragile or nonexistent. As part of this strategy, the Brotherhood sought to be a conduit for popular nationalist demands when state policy seemed to stray too far from popular opinion. An important example of this was relations with Israel, where the Brotherhood rejected Mubarak's mostly accommodationist stance. The Brotherhood's new strategy was part of its obsession with survival, which came to color the Mashour years. But it was also a reaction to the rise of new social classes—new upper and middle classes that emerged due to the capitalist opening and employment in the Gulf, as well as new lower classes that were largely employed in the informal economy.

The rise of Egypt's informal economy from the mid-1980s was the fundamental feature of the economy, and later at the core of the uprising in 2011. This was not simply the classical story of rural-urban migrations, but added to it was an oil boom in the Gulf which absorbed a sizable chunk of Egypt's working-age population (remittances from the diaspora accounted for 5 percent of GDP in 2016, and is currently the country's largest source of foreign earnings).[22] This capital inflow into the informal economy changed the structure of the middle and upper-middle classes, who until the early 1980s had considered a state job as the ultimate path to social mobility. A growing bourgeoisie was now correlated, not with incorporation into the fold of the state, but rather with being financially autonomous from it, and being a state employee soon became an indication of limited opportunities for mobility or prosperity. The marriage between informality and religious discourse was felt in the economy in the late 1980s when a few Salafi entrepreneurs capitalized on mistrust of formal financial institutions, alongside religious decrees that interest rates were a form of usury (prohibited by sharia), to form parallel banking companies known as "money investment companies" (*sharikat tawzif al-amwal*). Although the government later cracked down on these companies, their emergence signaled the presence of a new landscape in which the Brotherhood was not yet fully invested.[23]

Until the 1992 crackdown, the Brotherhood largely relied on incorporated classes, evident in its successes in syndicates and universities. This drastically changed in response to authoritarian pressure when the organization started focusing on surviving by using its social capital to expand among the social classes that were largely employed in the informal economy. Capital inflow into the informal economy created jobs in almost all industries throughout the Mubarak era. The informal economy included businesses and production in "commerce, agriculture, furniture, metal, and food processing, which operated entirely outside state laws and government control… Between 1980 and 2012, the informal economy grew consistently by 1 percent every year…[and] according to the World Bank, the informal economy reached 50 percent of the country's overall GDP."[24] The Brotherhood was now growing outside the political center by capitalizing on both the situation of financially autonomous middle and upper-middle classes and the informal working classes—for the former through dozens of top-quality schools, hospitals, and commercial projects providing what the ailing welfare state was not, along with satisfactory compliance with religion which the state was not considered trustworthy to provide, and for the working classes, through hundreds of charity initiatives and necessary services.

Contrary to the push for the institution of social justice through the state—a key element of Brotherhood discourse throughout the 1940s and early 1950s—the Brotherhood's remedies for poverty after the 1980s were to develop its own parallel networks of services.[25] The informal universe was seen as a boon for the organization to create what would become a fortress along the "fault lines" of the nation-state, and among the classes whom the state was incapable of integrating politically and pulling out of poverty. In the end, it was not hard to sell the model of a civil society organization providing services and basic commodities instead of the state in a nascent neoliberal era where the classical state was supposedly on the wane. That the regime chose to push the Brotherhood to the informal margins while tightening its grip on the sociopolitical center was a fair division of labor at a moment when it had no stamina to offer a serious developmental model. This strategy, in a largely centralized state, ultimately weakened the Brotherhood despite allowing it to quantitatively maximize its popular base at the margins.

The same informal logic applied to the relatively thin yet affluent bourgeoisie, which was left to survive on its own: its fortunes were barely touched by taxes and it had no representation in decision-making processes. The decade leading up to the uprising was characterized by an unprecedented weakening of the nation-state in ways that may be hard to conceptualize for the typical western observer. Parallel secluded spheres came to be carved and sub-identities flourished for many social groups; this was not specific to the Brotherhood. A westernized and liberal segment of the upper class came to have its own social and economic projects. Several Coptic spheres emerged as well, for the rich as well as the poor. Many schools, hospitals, charities, summer vacation spots, and sometimes even hairdressing shops, were known for their affiliation with either conservative Muslims, Brotherhood members, Salafis, Copts, or liberals. This fragmentation had its impact on the discourse of the

Brotherhood, especially within its own ranks, who were by the late 1990s keener than ever on intermarriage, sending their kids to their own schools, investing in their own projects, and so on. Although the Brotherhood continued to push as much as they could to maintain a presence in the syndicates, and maintained its presence and recruitment among university students, these groups were gradually marginalized within the Brotherhood, which was starting to lose its character as a national organization. Rather, it was transforming into a relatively secluded socioeconomic sphere for a thin upper-middle class, loosely connected to marginalized groups through a plethora of services along the fault lines of the nation-state.

The reshuffled base of the Brotherhood was crystal clear when the country had its first opportunity for a democratic election in 2012, revealing how the sociopolitical balance had evolved after the 1990s. Despite significant Brotherhood presence in the key Delta provinces closest to Cairo (Minufiyya, Gharbiyya, and Sharqiyya), the Mubarak regime's nexus of patronage was strongest in this part of Egypt, and Shafiq—Mubarak's last prime minister—came out as its favorite candidate. The results in Minufiyya, which usually has its share of political jokes for being the birthplace of Sadat and Mubarak, were quite striking, with Shafiq managing to win more than 50 percent of the votes in the competitive first round. Sharqiyya, Morsi's hometown, unexpectedly slipped to Shafiq as well by a thin margin in the first round, and by almost 160,000 votes in the second. It was no surprise, of course, that Morsi had his strongest showing in most Upper Egyptian provinces, in the marginalized rural provinces, notably Beni Suef and Fayoum, and in Egypt's second largest province by population, Giza, which includes a large "rural" fringe with swathes of informal housing. Morsi came on top in the first round as well among Egyptians living abroad, followed by the former Brotherhood member Aboul Fotouh and the Nasserist candidate Sabahi, while Shafiq came last with less than 10 percent.[26] Overall, the results indicated a rather moderate presence for the Brotherhood in Egypt's urban centers. (This contrasts markedly with the strong showing of Turkey's Justice and Development Party (AKP) in the country's cosmopolitan centers until 2015, a factor that enhanced its strength negotiating with Turkey's military, and made a coup plot harder to execute).

The Brotherhood's Fortress

Through the late 1990s and into the 2000s, the Brotherhood's new strategy provided it with a kind of fortress that ensured its social survival and expanding membership, but meant that political ambition took a back seat. From the late 1990s onward, the Brotherhood's political engagement with the regime was largely limited to utilizing the public space when the state gave it a green light for limited opposition (such as for protests for Palestine or Iraq); negotiating the organization's diminished influence in syndicates and associations; and protecting student networks in universities. In contrast, the Brotherhood's central power in the 1980s was its ability to contest the state within its corporatist institutions.

Although the Brotherhood's activities appeared relatively politically complacent throughout the 1990s and into the early 2000s, below the surface, it remained in a bitter political struggle with the regime, which cracked down on the Brotherhood's presence in the syndicates and universities. The Brotherhood also continued to seek to maximize its power in ways that fell short of direct confrontation, capitalizing on the weaknesses of the state in certain areas, speaking out when the state reneged on nationalism, and offering services where the state was almost nonexistent.

The Brotherhood's obsession with organizational survival paid off, as it carved up a parallel social sphere to which it could tactically withdraw during intense spats with the regime. This fortress mentality often correlated with—and was even ideologically perpetuated by—a Salafi-ized Qutbist narrative that glorified staying aloof from "rotten politics," partly by invoking Qutb's anti-modernism. Tilmisani's moderate conservatism was eclipsed by a resurgent nonviolent interpretation of Qutb's works, and this ideological shift befit the changes in the Brotherhood after 1992, when it was dominated by former Special Apparatus men who revered Qutb's ideas. This paradigm was also propagated by Muslim Brotherhood members of upper-middle and middle-class backgrounds, who looked at the Brotherhood as a safe haven from the "tyranny of the modern state." Non-Brotherhood thinkers and activists of this period who held Qutb in high esteem for his revolutionism and critiques of modernity also promoted the paradigm. Qutb was—supposedly—hanged because of his books in 1966, but by the late 1990s, those same books were readily available on the shelves of Egypt's most famous and liberal bookstore, Al-Shorouk. By this time, many of Qutb's most avid readers were affluent and educated.

The obsession with short-term tactics to survive, and the relative demise of long-term political strategizing on a national scale, would prove problematic after 2011, and indeed started to sow the seeds of what Mohammad Affan calls the depoliticization of the Brotherhood.[27] In its desire to maintain its fortress, the Brotherhood lost not only its identity as a national party, but also its capacity as a political actor vying for power at the center. Although the organization is usually blamed by friends and foes alike for this transformation, it is clear that its strategy served it well, in some ways, under Mubarak's authoritarian rule, especially in light of its priorities at the time.

On the other hand, the conservative religious trends within the Brotherhood also contributed to some of its depoliticization, even if its embrace of these trends was also partly a matter of survival. A decade before the uprising, the Brotherhood marginalized its vibrant political activists of universities and syndicates at the behest of a conservative administrative clique increasingly acceding to a populist Salafi mode of religiosity. The Brotherhood's competition with Salafism increasingly overshadowed the Brotherhood's other activities, not least because the Brotherhood and Salafis had intersecting constituencies at the margins of Egyptian society. This competition increasingly played out at the expense of the Brotherhood's original religious ideology.

Omar Hussein, a former Brotherhood student leader, recalled that some Brotherhood members began warning their colleagues against reading former reformist Brotherhood intellectuals who displayed awareness of national and modern politics, such as Mohammed al-Ghazali and Yusuf al-Qaradawi, for being "too open-minded."[28] Ghazali and Qaradawi are the two most famous Al-Azhar clerics to become members of the Brotherhood at some point in their lives, before choosing to part ways with the organization for different reasons. Their relatively moderate discourses, published throughout the 1980s onward, testify that membership in the Brotherhood—as a modern political organization—was a source of moderation and acceptance of political modernity until the late 1980s. It was only with its response to authoritarian pressures in 1992 and afterward that the organization chose to build a stronger fortress for its social power, and consequently appease the strong Salafi ideology dominating its new target audience.

The turn to Salafism spelled the end of the Brotherhood's near-total dominance of the religious conservatism of the professional middle classes, where Salafism had always been a minor force, just at the moment when a new wave of globalization was allowing new forms of bourgeois religiosity and religious thought to emerge.

No Longer a Religious Lodestar

From the 1970s onward, the Muslim Brotherhood had predicated its existence on being the vanguard of religious resurgence, which encompassed the social reconstitution of rituals such as mass prayers and women putting on the hijab, alongside an "alms" economy which was key to its social power. In the 2000s, however, the gradual ideological recession of the Brotherhood—especially among the affluent middle class—was a significant blow to the organization. The case of televangelist Amr Khaled is indicative. A former Brotherhood member from the affluent Mohandeseen neighborhood in Greater Cairo, Khaled rose to stratospheric popularity as a televangelist in the early 2000s, with his own show, broadcast on a Saudi network. He became an icon for a new mode of apolitical religiosity that was more in line with the regime's diktats. Khaled's rise was welcomed by the Brotherhood as a "Brother" helping fellow Muslims adhere to their creed. But the love was unrequited. Khaled had a keen understanding of the national political calculus—especially after founding a large charitable organization named Sunna'a al-Haya (Life Makers)—and distanced himself from the Brotherhood to avoid the regime's anger.[29]

There are several other cases from this period indicating that the Brotherhood was losing its influence over the religious narrative. The oil boom in the Gulf after 2003 galvanized new forms of religious discourse, most importantly the private Saudi satellite channels Iqraa and Al-Resalah (names meaning Read and The Message, respectively) with strong religious overtones, alongside Sharjah TV (which was owned by the emirate of Sharjah in the United Arab Emirates, and had connections to Islamist preachers). The Doha-based IslamOnline website (IslamOnline.net) also grew in influence. The Gulf countries had a new, sudden interest in crafting new religious narratives, in response to post-9/11 American demands to curtail Islamist radicalism. The Brotherhood, which saw itself as a classical Islamist organization, did not take sufficient moves to take a side in the Global War on Terror discourse. It did not try to take advantage of the American opening to moderate Islamism by posing as a moderate religious party (as the Justice and Development Party in Turkey did), aside from gestures from its affiliates abroad that it was not a violent organization. But neither did the Brotherhood cement its now-populist and Salafi-ized Islamist base, because it wanted to avoid both escalation with the regime and being perceived as an extremist group in the West.

The Brotherhood's narrative regarding the Taliban, for instance, was blurred, as scholar Heba Ezzat describes. It made a half-hearted defense of the Taliban as a victim of imperialism, without questioning its alliance with al-Qaeda.[30] The Brotherhood saw anti-Americanism, which had long been a tool utilized by both the regime and Islamist movements when expedient, as an important element of its popular power, even if the organization's leaders themselves were not necessarily anti-American. During the War on Terror, the leadership calculated that if it took a bold step to open up to the United States—much like the Justice and Development Party had done in Turkey at the time—it would induce not only the wrath of the regime, but also accusations in official media outlets that the group was a stooge for American imperialism. This fear of losing anti-American ground to the regime was not unfounded, as later events exemplified when the Brotherhood became a target of anti-Americanism during the populist campaign against it in 2013, after the organization showed serious willingness to engage with the United States.

In general, the Brotherhood's narrative zigzagged between radical positions to appease its populist base at the margins, and more moderate reformist ideas to contain the middle classes at the center and project a positive image to the West. The result was that the Brotherhood's real intentions remained unclear for a large segment of educated Egyptians, even those who sympathized with it on the grounds of religiosity. The Brotherhood continued to insist throughout the 2000s that it was open to a modern democratic and constitutional government, and repeatedly gave assurances that it was not bent on transforming Egypt into another Iran or Sudan. On the other hand, and knowing how cultural and religious issues remained key for its conservative base, it continued to stress that the role of women is first and foremost in their household, a position that remained largely unchanged, culminating in the drafting of a constitution in 2012 with an emphasis on so-called family values. For instance, Saad el-Katatni, a senior Guidance Bureau member who was usually a voice of moderation, stated in 2008 that banning female circumcision "runs counter to the norms, customs, and nature of the Egyptian people."[31] Although it is hard to believe that any of the prominent Brotherhood families upheld female circumcision as a practice themselves, Katatni was clearly toeing the line of a conservative rural public sentiment in a country where female circumcision continues to be a normal procedure outside urban centers. Once again, the Brotherhood opted to distance itself from a progressive position that would have appealed to its middle-class members in order to appease its rural popular base.

An Aversion to Progressive Ideas

Throughout the two decades prior to 2011, the Brotherhood developed an aversion to progressive ideas. It associated Marxism with atheism, and progressive ideas in general with the "lax" lifestyle of those who propagated them. The Brotherhood came to be obsessed with secularism, rather than authoritarianism, which had shaped the ideas of the older generation who had gone through Nasser's oppression and later bitter clashes with leftists and communists. Prominent questions were largely about women and the veil, interest rates, irreligious forms of art, alcohol, and tourism, or whether democracy and pluralism are compatible with sharia.[32]

But even as the Brotherhood's leadership turned away from progressivism, a new generation of the Brotherhood was molded by its enmity for security agents on university campuses. This generation was more open to Western and reformist ideas about confronting the authoritarianism of the regime. Indeed, several ideas circulated among the youth of the Islamist intelligentsia arguing that the Anglo-American style of secularism, which honors the public role of religion, was acceptable—unlike French laicism. Abdel-Wahab

El-Messiri, a popular Marxist-turned-Islamist thinker of this period, was famous for his two-volume work titled *Partial Secularism and Comprehensive Secularism*—the former being the mild and, for him, acceptable form.[33] Although many Islamist and post-Islamist youth would later criticize what they saw as Messiri's shallow engagement with the concept of secularism, it was by the early 2000s established among many young Islamists that the clash with secular forces—largely marginal in Egypt—was a clash of a bygone era, and that the real threat to the Islamic resurgence was the tyranny of the regime.

The regime itself, acquiescing to the fact that resurgent religiosity had become mainstream, began to propagate apolitical forms of religiosity to compete with Islamist preachers and scholars, particularly from the 1990s onward. The most famous such voice at the time was Sheikh Muhammad Metwalli al-Sha'rawi, an apolitical Al-Azhar scholar who kept a distance from the regime without discussing politics, and who presented spiritual readings of the Quran. The ideological contest was becoming one between Islamist religiosity versus quietist religiosity. For their part, older Brotherhood leaders continued to view their social capital through the narrow prism of religious-versus-secular, leading them to overestimate the size of their following by assuming that mere religiosity was a guaranteed vote at the ballot box. As such, religiosity occupied center stage in the ideological foundation of the Brotherhood, obliterating any clear social or political ideology.

With the technological revolution of the early 2000s, and the rapid expansion of mobile phone use and computers coupled with Internet access, a generation of reformist Islamists came to dominate among middle class students. This generation brought to the Islamist conversation more complex intellectual ideas, along with a renewed interest in humanities, reform, and questions of modernity and the nation-state. Some of these thinkers actually joined the Brotherhood, though they faced disappointment and exclusion after the revolution. It was mainly within a small group of Islamic intellectuals that a new discourse was developing during the 2000s, and although they managed to heal the rift between progressive ideas and religion, their impact was limited to a thin stratum of the educated middle class. The impact, however, was qualitatively effective, especially on university campuses.[34]

The emergence of a bourgeois Islamic public sphere was not a definitive eclipse of the Brotherhood in an ideological sense, because the new voices largely retained current or past links to the Brotherhood. Nevertheless, this Islamic caucus existed beyond the confines of the Brotherhood as an organization. It came to be more effective at expanding Islamic conservatism, whether it was imbued with sympathy for the Brotherhood or not, and this effect reduced the political dominance of the Brotherhood. This democratization and decentralization of Islamic ideology meant that the Brotherhood was increasingly becoming a sociopolitical interest group, while its generic resurgent religiosity had already become mainstream and too widespread to constitute any useful, demarcated political ideology. In short, the Islamic resurgence was a social success, but it posed a political question about what role the Brotherhood would play in a largely religious society where different social segments were rallying for their divergent interests in the context of a weakening of the Mubarak regime and a wave of sociopolitical discontent.

Interviewees described Quranic study circles on college campuses that were prime recruiting grounds for the Brotherhood; student activities devoted to religious rituals were mainstays of the Brotherhood's recruitment strategy.[35] The focus on such activities was successful in recruiting a more diverse membership, with people from different social classes and regions of Egypt standing "shoulder to shoulder," in the words of one interviewee, within campus Brotherhood affiliates.[36] But the fluid and apolitical nature of religiosity made it quite impossible for the organization to conceptualize itself as an interest group in any solid form or to claim a coherent ideological program. Taking personal religiosity as an index of support or potential support for the Brotherhood was a relic of the 1970s, and the Brotherhood did not understand that. By the 2000s and certainly after the revolution, it was too generic to constitute a viable political classification.

At the same time that the Brotherhood's ideological frailty was being exposed, it bungled its attempts at adapting to the ascendant neoliberal global order, further exposing fractures in the organization. Given that the Brotherhood's administrative structure largely mimicked that of the state, it was not surprising that an apolitical managerial turn was ongoing within the ranks of the Brotherhood concomitant with the same shift taking place within the regime.

During the premiership of Ahmed Nazif (2004–2011), Mubarak took a neoliberal turn and included successful businessmen in the ruling party and cabinet, and additionally made efforts to address the failures of the post-Nasserist bureaucracy. The Brotherhood too put forward apolitical managerial reforms during this period. Led by Khairat al-Shater, the structural shake-up was intended to free the Brotherhood from the shackles of its erstwhile syndicalist generation, molded by years of student activism and partially representational politics throughout the 1970s and 1980s.[37] This policy seemed sound at the time, due to the diminishing weight of the Egyptian middle class, from which Brotherhood professionals were drawn. The Brotherhood leadership sought to capitalize on new sources of power, which were assumed to be the twin of its commercial capital and a popular Salafi-ized base.

There was a political-economic factor at play as well. While the rift between conservatives and reformists was often portrayed as inherently ideological, it largely straddled a socioeconomic crack between professionals and businessmen who barely had interests in common and were united only by general Islamic inclinations. Student activists and syndicalists tended to occupy a rather center or center-of-left inclination, whereas the clique of merchants and businessmen at the helm of the Brotherhood occupied the right end of the political spectrum.

(After the 2011 revolution, these two poles were represented by the Wasat Party and Abdel Moneim Aboul Fotouh's presidential campaign, on the left, and Mohamed Morsi, on the right.)

Indeed, Brotherhood leader and businessman Hassan Malek stated in late 2011 that the Brotherhood had no reservations about the economic policies of Mubarak's last cabinet, but simply opposed the corruption of the businessmen affiliated with it.[38] This was a rather ill-timed statement given that the accumulating discontent was clearly about much more than corruption, a mainstay of Egypt's economy for decades. Corruption was entangled with many aspects of Nazif's neoliberal policies, which had drawn the ire of workers and ushered in an unprecedented wave of workers' strikes before 2011. Malek's comments can be seen as part of the Brotherhood's wider effort to project an image of itself as a conservative force that would not upend the political and economic status quo, and would not concede to the uprising's more revolutionary demands. The statement also exemplified the gap between the Muslim Brotherhood's priorities and the mounting political discontent in Egypt.

A Growing Dissonance

In the run-up to the 2005 parliamentary elections, Brotherhood supporters marched down a boulevard in the affluent eastern Cairo neighborhood of Heliopolis, in a show of support for one of their candidates. "Tiba! Tiba!" they chanted, using an Egyptian pronunciation for one of the names of the holy city of Medina. They hoped to galvanize supporters by calling to mind a time, in the early days of Islam, when Medina provided a refuge for the Prophet Mohammed when he was chased out of Mecca.

For many onlookers, however, the chant simply produced confusion: Tiba is also the name of an old capital city along the Nile in ancient Egypt, and is used as a shorthand for Egypt as motherland; most educated Egyptians would think of this meaning of Tiba. As a shorthand for the Prophet's haven, Taybah (and much more so, Tiba) was relatively limited in modern Islamic discourse and popular preaching. The residents of Heliopolis could merely scratch their heads. This moment of incongruity epitomized the gap between the energetic Brotherhood youth and large segments of Egyptian society.[39]

Incidents such as these in the years leading up to the uprising are key in understanding how the Brotherhood's responses to authoritarian pressure, although successful within its social strongholds, situated it in an unfavorable sociopolitical position overall when the uprising erupted. There was a growing dissonance between the Brotherhood's leadership and part of its ranks on one hand, and the rising popular discontent against the regime on the other hand. This dissonance is one of the most important features of Brotherhood activism throughout this period.

The organization put in place a solid centralized hierarchy in 2005, and announced a controversial party platform in 2007. The platform included measures such as barring women and Christians from running as presidential candidates and instituting an independent committee for "senior religious scholars" to play a supervisory role over both parliament and the presidency.[40] Once again, the Brotherhood program was primarily aimed at its constituency, and successfully communicated its conservative ideology to them. It received criticisms, however, from many educated Egyptians, including young Brotherhood members, alongside independent Islamic scholars and activists, most famously Qaradawi.[41] Although the release of the program reflected the desire of the Brotherhood to resuscitate its interest in politics and to politically define itself, the mixed messages from various constituencies and negative reactions from both non-Islamists and reformist Islamists forced it to withdraw the program altogether.

The pattern of initiating political action to test the waters with regard to a more overt political role, only to withdraw or adjust it to adapt to criticisms or evade political pressure might have, at times, shown the Brotherhood's flexibility. At other times, however, it indicated the extent to which the organization lacked a coherent political ideology, and that its strategy was simply to check to see which way the wind was blowing before doing anything politically assertive. This pattern of behavior became more pronounced, and problematic, after 2011.

More Political Retreat

The Brotherhood enjoyed a brief opening of the political climate in Egypt between 2003 and 2007. Its new leader, Mohammed Mahdi Akef (general guide 2004–10), was able to take advantage of this opening and he revived the Brotherhood's national consensual politics. Under his leadership, the Brotherhood contributed to the Egypt-wide Kifaya movement, which opposed Mubarak's presidency and grew out of initiatives supporting the Palestinian intifada in 2001 and opposing the war in Iraq in 2003. The Brotherhood also participated in the National Association for Change, which was launched in the aftermath of a February 2010 meeting convened by Mohamed ElBaradei, and brought together a diverse group of politicians and intellectuals to push for change in Egypt.[42] These moves were limited to specific causes, however, and did not signal broader political participation on the part of the Brotherhood. Furthermore, when the Brotherhood released its new draft party program in 2007, it did little to reduce the perception shared by many Egyptians that the Brotherhood favored an Iran-like religious regime. The release of the platform stemmed from the Brotherhood's desire to engage in politics, but it was ultimately unhelpful in positioning the Brotherhood as a serious political player.

A renewed crackdown on the Brotherhood started with military trials in 2007, and the Brotherhood was back on the defensive. Faced with another round of authoritarian pressure, the Brotherhood's response was—again—to solidify its grip on its internal structures.

These developments coincided with massive worker strikes and new forms of student activism, the likes of which had not occurred in Egypt since the mid-1970s. The Brotherhood, however, was not fully in touch with this new wave of discontent. Instead, it focused on avoiding escalation with the Mubarak regime—no matter how much the regime increased the pressure. This avoidance defined the politics of the Brotherhood—or, more accurately, its gradual withdrawal from politics—in the few years leading up to the uprising. Additionally, the Brotherhood remained relatively socially secluded, as it had since Mubarak's first crackdown began in 1992. This seclusion did not help in reading the popular mood or properly strategizing for confronting the regime when the time came.

In 2010, state oppression of the Brotherhood intensified further, and it was clear that the organization was once again withdrawing to its survival fortress. This withdrawal coincided with the choice of Mohammed Badie as general guide. The new leadership failed to convince the Brotherhood youth, led by a group of young bloggers (which included one of this book's authors, Abdelrahman Ayyash), who challenged the organization's die-hard conservatism.[43] Many Brotherhood members came to be involved in this new Internet-based activism and contributed to a new intelligentsia that stood at the heart of the political events during the years prior to 2011. The Brotherhood leadership did not understand their initiative, however. (A very indicative illustration of the leadership's cluelessness is the 2007 meeting it had with bloggers, Ayyash included, described in the preface to this book.) Openly protesting the regime, too, was out of the question: "The street is a red line," was how Amir recalled the orders of senior Brotherhood members warning Brotherhood members against anti-regime protest.[44]

The gap between the leadership and the more progressive Brotherhood youth became pronounced during the revolution. On February 4, 2011, while hundreds of thousands continued to flock into Tahrir Square, news circulated on a small scale about a meeting between several political figures (including Brotherhood leaders) and Mubarak's general intelligence chief, Omar Suleiman. Given the mood at the square, it was hardly surprising that many Brotherhood members did not support this meeting. For instance, Islam Lotfi, a former student leader of the Brotherhood, refused to attend the meeting despite a phone call from Morsi to bring him to the table.[45]

Brotherhood members were not simply present at the encampments of Tahrir Square but also active in the revolution—famously, they played a heroic role defending protesters during the so-called Battle of the Camel on February 2. But the political position of the Brotherhood's leadership continued to be obsessed with survival—indicating that it was out of touch with the tectonic shifts underway in the country.

On February 11, 2011, hours before Mubarak's resignation was announced, a group of Brotherhood members met in a hotel near Tahrir Square. Lotfi, who attended the meeting along with senior Brotherhood members, recalled that a Guidance Bureau member warned attendees not to adopt a position that would be seen as an "escalation" by the Mubarak regime. This warning was a grim caricature of the Brotherhood's excessive risk-aversion: at this point, even SCAF knew—as did many others—that the Mubarak regime was almost at its end, even if state institutions were largely intact. SCAF released a statement at noon on February 11 suspending the state of emergency and announcing its intention to carry out constitutional amendments and fresh presidential elections, referring to the protests as "the current successive events that will decide the destiny of the country." A few hours later, Vice President Omar Suleiman was beamed to televisions and computers around the world, in a hastily thrown-together set to announce Mubarak's resignation. It was clear that the Brotherhood leadership was at least a few steps behind the momentum of events.

The detachment from a public sentiment that was diffusing among its students and urban members beyond the tiny ring of decision-makers had its impact on the organization in the aftermath of the uprising. According to a study by Yasser Fathy, based on extensive interviews with current and former Brotherhood members, only 17 percent were critical of SCAF in February 2011 amid a seeming Brotherhood–SCAF entente. By late 2011, however, 79 percent of Brotherhood members expressed support for campaigns against SCAF. Interviews with Brotherhood student leaders in the study revealed that they refrained from communicating Brotherhood orders to stay away from protests against SCAF during the Mohammed Mahmoud Street events in November 2011. Brotherhood student leaders made such decisions all across the country even though they had made no prior agreement to ignore Brotherhood orders, because they sought to avoid the ire of students who had become critical of SCAF's rule and wanted to join the protests in Tahrir. These were improvised decisions made independently by student leaders in several universities.[46]

In March 2012, the Brotherhood decided to nominate a presidential candidate, Mohamed Morsi, after previous pledges not to make a nomination. The Brotherhood had signaled that it was not intending to contest the presidential elections, so as to avoid a perception that it was rushing to dominate state institutions. The Brotherhood justified its reversal of this position by pointing to what it saw as SCAF's moves to strangle parliament, which had been the nexus of Brotherhood power after the November 2011 parliamentary elections. Fathy's study shows surprisingly limited support for Morsi among Brotherhood members at the beginning of the presidential campaign, with only 27 percent supporting Morsi's nomination, while 63 percent supported a non-Brotherhood candidate—most probably Aboul Fotouh, whose campaign attracted a sizeable segment of disgruntled Brotherhood youth. By the time of the election, however, these early preferences had evaporated, with 61 percent saying they voted for Morsi, while only 2 percent reported that they voted for a non-Brotherhood candidate. Organizational loyalty, it seems, remained strong even among critical Brothers.

The Brotherhood's sudden shift to seek the highest political office after earlier promises that it was going to share power ("Sharing not domination" was a famous Brotherhood slogan at the time), was seen by many as a sign of impending monopolization of power. The Brotherhood's bid for the presidency was motivated less by a thirst for power than fear of being exterminated by a new regime, however.

A further key factor was inter-Islamist competition, which left the organization wary that another Islamist nomination would garner the votes of Brotherhood sympathizers. When Hazem Salah Abu Ismail, a popular Salafi lawyer and preacher, nominated himself and attracted thousands of ultraconservative Egyptians, the Brotherhood's fears about inter-Islamist competition were vindicated. Abu Ismail's candidacy was also an indicator that the Islamist street was too fluid to be under the command of one organization, and that the Brotherhood was on the verge of losing its social capital to a competitor if did not cater to the popular desire for an "Islamic president." Although the earlier assumption was that not putting forward a candidate would allow the Brotherhood to gain the trust of state institutions and those who accused it of seeking domination, it was now clear that such a move had a hefty cost. This moment appears to have put the organization under pressure to move to the right, centering its Islamic credentials during the presidential elections and drafting of the constitution, and allying with the Salafis in parliament. Alongside its fear of a renewed wave of oppression, the Brotherhood's strategy was shaped by the competitive pressure represented by the presence of hardline rivals in the Islamic public sphere. These two concerns often led to contradictory policies and mixed messages to the public.

In one of the instances that exemplified the Brotherhood's confused relationship with Egypt's public sphere, particularly after its sudden expansion after 2011, the newly elected president Morsi spoke to crowds about how repressive Nasser's era was. Needless to say, most of Egypt's population at that moment had not lived through the 1960s, and much of the working-class continued to look at the Nasser era as a benchmark for nationalism and social welfare. Morsi's explicit warning about the 1960s soon became a sarcastic reference. Just a few months later, Morsi applauded Nasser's industrialization efforts on Labor Day during a visit to the country's infamous steel factories in Helwan, south of Cairo, while pledging to "resume what Nasser began."[47] This zigzagging was not particular to domestic politics and historical narratives, but extended to regional politics, most importantly with regard to Turkey and Iran.

Sectarianism and Jihad

In August 2012, Morsi went to Tehran to attend the Non-Aligned Movement summit, and in February 2013, Mahmoud Ahmadinejad was in Cairo for the Islamic Summit of the Organisation of Islamic Cooperation. These visits were described as historic, as they indicated that Egypt was finally opening to Iran after years of cold relations under Mubarak. Morsi also proposed the formation of a "contact group" bringing together Egypt, Saudi Arabia, Turkey, and Iran to discuss regional issues. This was understood by some analysts as an implicit rejection by the Brotherhood of sectarianizing Egypt's foreign policy along Sunni lines.[48]

By June 2013, however, Morsi had acquiesced to populist Salafism and the sectarian approach of the Gulf countries toward Iran and Syria. At an event organized by Islamist parties at the Cairo Stadium, Morsi announced Egypt would be cutting relations with Syria's Assad and pledged support for the Syrian uprising.[49] He stood on stage in front of thousands of supporters and alongside a group of Salafi preachers, senior Brotherhood members, and leaders of al-Gama'a al-Islamiyya. Senior attendees publicly vowed to support jihad in Syria; these included a Salafi preacher with ties to Saudi Arabia who urged Arab counties not to impede the flow of fighters to aid those fighting Assad. Two days earlier, at a meeting in a Cairo hotel attended by Islamists and Salafi leaders, Safwat Hegazy, a prominent preacher with ties to the Brotherhood, declared Assad, his regime, and Hezbollah to be "infidels."

Interestingly, Egypt's *Al-Youm Al-Sabe'* newspaper reported a potential spat around this time between Qaradawi and preacher Salah Sultan, also with ties to the Brotherhood. Sultan reportedly urged Qaradawi to expel Shia scholars from the International Union of Muslim Scholars (IUMS), which he chaired at the time.[50] The IUMS, known for its ties to the Brotherhood, had been vocal in its support of Hezbollah during its 2006 war with Israel. This earlier stance had pitted the IUMS against Salafi scholars close to Saudi Arabia, who were critical of Hezbollah's role in Lebanon (even if there was no love lost for Israel). As a wave of sympathy with Hezbollah had overwhelmed the Arab world, these scholars had been more focused on highlighting doctrinal differences between Sunni and Shia Muslims.[51]

Later, the Brotherhood also turned against Hezbollah. Of course, after 2011, the Lebanese militant group lost much of its luster in the Arab world when it began helping the regime of Bashar al-Assad to suppress the revolution in Syria. Moderate Islamic activists everywhere were shocked by Hezbollah's violence against the Syrian people. The Brotherhood's turn, however, had more to do with its increased political alignment with Salafis, which was clearly overshadowing and undermining the Brotherhood's doctrinal perception of Shia as fellow Muslims. The Brotherhood was pushing itself further into a sectarian populist campaign where opposition to Assad was frequently mixed with anti-Shia sentiment, Saudi priorities, and jihadist forces.

The Brotherhood's new alignment with jihadist forces in Syria was especially alarming for SCAF, according to an Egyptian officer who spoke anonymously to Voice of America in July 2013.[52] SCAF was concerned given what had happened with past foreign jihads: Sadat had officially embraced sending zealous fighters to engage in jihad abroad after the Soviet invasion of Afghanistan. The hundreds of Egyptian jihadists who flocked to Afghanistan eventually returned home, and unleashed a wave of violence throughout the 1980s and 1990s. Since then, flirting with exporting jihadists had become a red line for the military. The Brotherhood's endorsement of exporting jihad to Syria in 2013 was thus a turning point in SCAF's perception of the Brotherhood.[53]

Again, the political fluidity of Morsi's presidency transformed the Brotherhood's tactics for seeking allies into a series of trials and errors. While some of these experiments earned the Brotherhood new allies, others eroded the understanding between the Brotherhood and SCAF—an understanding that was vital for the Brotherhood to maintain power. Dealing with the Salafi challenge was increasingly at odds with maintaining the trust of state institutions.

Incongruent and Fickle Allies

Similarly, Brotherhood hostility to Turkey's AKP, whose agenda it had at one time considered "secular and Westernizing," swiftly transformed into a tight alliance in 2013 and thereafter. During Recep Tayyip Erdogan's visit to Egypt in September 2011, Turkey's young and reformist (at the time) leader spoke in favor of a secular state ruling a Muslim society. The response from Essam al-Erian, a senior Brotherhood leader who was usually considered a reformist, was stern: "Neither Erdogan nor any other leader has the right to interfere in the affairs of another state and impose a certain model on it," he said. "The Egyptian people will not understand or accept any defense of a secular regime, even if it is the Turkish regime."[54] Once Morsi was in power, however, the relations between Cairo and Ankara quickly warmed.

Although analysts usually highlight the ideological resonances between the two parties (which have similar roots), ideology does not appear to have been the chief catalyst for the alliance during Morsi's tenure. After all, the Brotherhood had previously expressed its reservations on the AKP model, and was already in alliance with Salafi parties. The immense administrative experience the AKP had in Turkey may have motivated the Brotherhood to make it an ally once it found out that ruling the state and addressing governance issues was a daunting task. For the AKP, the alliance made sense given its support for the Arab uprisings and what Ankara perceived as moderate Islamists. While for the Brotherhood the alliance also made sense, it represented yet another zigzag in its policies.

Cozying up to Salafis did not bear fruit, however. Both the Brotherhood and SCAF were aware that they had to deal with the Salafis' strong popular presence. It was with the Brotherhood that the Salafis first developed tensions. The Salafi Call, an Egyptian organization founded in 1984, loathed politics since its inception, and had long had a critical view of the Brotherhood. This was not simply a matter of competition between two Islamic groups, but was driven by social and political differences. The Salafi Call was largely composed of non-professional lay preachers who grew in profile and number at the same time that Al-Azhar's traditional and professional nexus of clerics lost part of its appeal. The Brotherhood was, by nature, closer to the traditional clerics who were trying to reconcile traditional Islam and modernity, since it was led by classes that continued to respect the classical scholars.[55] The Brotherhood tended to represent middle and upper-middle class professionals, whereas the rapid expansion of Salafism in the 1970s had occurred mostly (though not exclusively) among the ranks of lower and lower-middle classes.

After the revolution, even as the Brotherhood became increasingly reliant on the Salafis, it often neglected these crucial social differences, while the Salafi Call did not. Indeed, tensions within the ranks of the Salafi Call revolved largely around whether to ally with the Brotherhood. Two factions emerged in the aftermath of the revolution, following the establishment of the Nour Party as an arm of the Salafi Call. One faction was led by Imad Abd al-Ghafour, a medical doctor who helped found the movement in the 1970s and was critical of its lack of engagement with revolution and politics. The other faction was led by Salafi lay preacher Yasir Burhami, alongside the religious sheikhs who stood at the helm of the Salafi Call movement. Abd al-Ghafour's position was strengthened with the success of the uprising in 2011, and he founded the Nour Party, although tensions with Burhami continued to cause strain.[56] In January 2013, Abd al-Ghafour left the party, effectively ceding it to Burhami. Afterward, tensions gradually increased between the Salafi Call and the Brotherhood, culminating in the presence of the Salafi Call in the televised broadcast announcing the coup against Morsi's presidency on July 3, 2013.[57]

The last of the Brotherhood allies to abandon it was al-Gama'a al-Islamiyya. Based primarily in Upper Egypt and historically less critical of doing politics, the group had been a power broker in Upper Egypt after its renunciation of violence in 1998. Al-Gama'a al-Islamiyya was willing to go far in its support of the Brotherhood, even effectively wresting control of a few provinces in Upper Egypt after the July 3 coup, presumably to raise the costs of SCAF using violence until an acceptable deal was reached.[58]

It appears that the Brotherhood lost al-Gama'a al-Islamiyya as an ally when it accommodated SCAF demands later that summer. According to Lotfi, several deals were struck behind closed doors between army generals and Brotherhood politicians, as protesters gathered in Rabaa al-Adawiya Square in the summer of 2013 to support ousted president Morsi. One such deal entailed the Brotherhood forfeiting the presidency and retaining only a 30 percent share in a future parliament and government. Badie, the general guide, reportedly accepted this deal, although more than one source has said that he later backed out of this and other deals. Amir cited Badie's inability to declare the deal before the gathering masses at the Rabaa sit-in, who seemed to have become a force of their own—again testifying to the fluid link between the Brotherhood and the populist wave it galvanized without commanding it in full.[59] Lotfi, on the other hand, did not consider the sit-in as consequential so much as the Brotherhood's lack of a negotiation strategy, which led even its Islamist allies to give up on it. Whether Badie indeed failed to communicate the deal to the restive masses, suddenly decided that he could get more when he saw them, or simply intended negotiations to be a tactic to buy time, the result was losing al-Gama'a al-Islamiyya as an ally. A few days after it seized control of several Upper Egyptian cities, the group quietly withdrew from its posts, effectively signaling to the army that its control was nominally back in place.

A Full Loss of Identity

As the Brotherhood stood bare except for its own social and political base—which proved less dominant and powerful than previously assumed—its position became precarious. The Brotherhood had not just lost its identity as a national party and its organizational capacity to play politics, but also the trust of two Islamic actors who had no political aspirations on a national scale. These actors were now willing to engage the military rather than sink with a project with which they had little in common as interest groups, save for beards and long veils.

In fact, the Brotherhood was the only party that lacked an identity as an interest group. It jerked across the political scene in an attempt to survive, hoarding supporters and political office, without offering a viable structural connection between the two. Those constituencies who were key to the 2011 uprising's success and were expected to reap its fruits as the Brotherhood presumably embarked on an ambitious "national" project, ultimately became the victims both of the Brotherhood's failure and the regime's reinvigorated authoritarianism.

It is hard to blame the organization for not foreseeing an uprising which was unforeseen by almost everyone. It remains true, however, that the tightened grip of the former Special Apparatus men, the group's failed attempt at creating a political platform, and the near depoliticization of the organization with the rise of Badie put the Brotherhood in a weak position when 2011 arrived. It was more difficult for the Brotherhood to understand the political scene, communicate with the public, or devise a sound political strategy, least of all in a short transitional period during which it was subject to conflicting pressures. The uprising presented the Brotherhood with a social reality that it could not get to grips with because it had been relatively socially isolated for two decades. The new reality gradually exposed the shortcomings of the tactics the Brotherhood had employed during the Mubarak era. The organization was in an unenviable position, having to reckon with so many shifts and new parameters when its solid conservative ethos provided it with little tools to effectively do so.

At the same time, Egypt's largest social organization could not remain aloof from the contest for power. It had to engage in this contest less out of hunger for power and rather as a hedge against unfriendly forces rising to dominance, including Islamist competitors. The political mission that the Brotherhood had always aspired to undertake, and had learned along the years to give up for the sake of its survival, finally presented itself when the Brotherhood was least ready.

2
The Legitimacy Crisis

Two Brotherhood members were walking in a protest of a million people. One asked the other, "Are we going in the right direction?" The other responded: "Can't you see those two leaders in the front? They know where we're heading and I'm sure they're going in the right direction." The two leaders were also talking and one asked the other, "Are we going in the right direction?" The other pointed to the million followers and said, "Do you see all of them? They wouldn't have followed us if we weren't right."

—A joke told by a former Brotherhood student leader

By Any Means Necessary?

On August 28, 2020, the Egyptian Ministry of Interior announced that its forces had arrested Mahmoud Ezzat, the acting general guide of the Muslim Brotherhood, who had been considered the most influential of those who used to be described as the movement's hawks.[1] Ezzat was the last top leader of the Brotherhood's Guidance Bureau to be arrested despite being on the top of the government's most-wanted list for years. A medical professor, Ezzat had served as secretary-general of the movement before 2009 and deputy chairman since the internal elections of 2009. He automatically took the position of acting general guide after the arrest of Mohammed Badie, the previous general guide, in August 2013, as according to the Brotherhood's bylaws, the eldest member of the Guidance Bureau not in prison should assume this responsibility.

The Brotherhood had witnessed several crises that split the movement vertically, but Ezzat and his faction were able to control the movement and to defuse internal opposition to his leadership. Thus, it seemed relatively in keeping with the Brotherhood's history of resilience when it issued a statement following his arrest saying that "its day-to-day activities will continue normally and institutionally without being affected by the absence of any of their leaders."[2]

This statement was far from the truth, however. In the months that followed Ezzat's detainment, the movement was split in ways that affected its day-to-day affairs, leadership, and rank and file. For external observers, the rapid divisions that appeared in the body of the Brotherhood revealed how fragile the organization that Ezzat led really was. But for people on the inside, many of these changes were a long time coming.

The Shock (July 2013 to July 2015)

In the aftermath of the Rabaa Massacre of August 14, 2013, which left hundreds of Brotherhood members and supporters dead, Ezzat, the newly-appointed general guide, vanished off the radar of both the state and the Brotherhood. Nevertheless, the heavily centralized movement continued its activities in an impressively decentralized manner. The Muslim Brotherhood is not, as some would claim, a Mafia-like organization in a sense that it cannot function if "decapitated."[3] Several interviewees reported that weekly usra meetings resumed throughout the country just a month after the massacre, in what was a heavily surveilled and securitized period. Further, anti-coup demonstrations and activities continued despite the severed connections between the base and the leaders. These, however, lacked strategy, as they were impulsive actions motivated by psychological shock, feelings of anger, and a desire for revenge after the massacre and an unprecedented security crackdown.[4]

Only three of the twenty Guidance Bureau members were able to organize and resume their responsibilities as leaders of the movement, as the rest were either imprisoned, in hiding, or abroad. All three leaders had joined the Guidance Bureau recently: Mohamed Kamal in August 2011, Mohamed Taha Wahdan in February 2012, and Mohammed Saad Eliwa in January 2013.[5] Most members of the Guidance Bureau had joined many years earlier, such as Mahmoud Ezzat, former deputy chairman Khairat al-Shater, the former general guide Mohammed Mahdi Akef, and the then-secretary-general Mahmoud Ghozlan, all of whom were elected in 1995. As recent arrivals, Kamal, Wahdan, and Eliwa were not part of what could be called the "historical leadership" of the organization. In February 2014, after months of organizational disarray, the three leaders convened those members of the General Shura Council who had not been arrested and established an entity to replace the Guidance Bureau in leading the movement: the High Administrative Committee (HAC). The HAC consisted of at least nine members and included three second-tier leaders: Ali Bateekh, the head of one of the administrative offices in Cairo; Hussein Ibrahim, a former member of parliament and a leader in the Brotherhood's political arm the Freedom and Justice Party (FJP); and Abdelfattah Ibrahim al-Sisi, a General Shura Council member and a member of the Central Upbringing Committee. Sisi was chosen to be the secretary-general of the HAC. This position enabled him to follow the day-to-day activities of the movement all over the country and to have direct connections with active Brotherhood members across membership levels, though these interactions were limited due to security concerns. In effect, this position made Sisi one of the most powerful Brotherhood figures in Egypt.

The International Organization

Outside Egypt, however, the scene was somewhat different. For many years, the Brotherhood has had many chapters throughout the world.

The group's leaders often stated that the Brotherhood was active in more than eighty countries.[6] Naturally, the international element of the Brotherhood was reflected in the structure of the movement.

The affairs of the Brotherhood outside Egypt are run by two structures. First is the International Organization (*al-Tanzim al-Dawli*) made up of elected leadership from every country where the Brotherhood is present. These elected leaders answer and report to the Brotherhood's general guide. The International Organization is run from London. Its secretary-general was, until his death in late 2022, Ibrahim Munir (b. 1937), a lawyer who spent more than fourteen years in Egyptian prisons between 1955 and 1972.

The second structure is the Association of Egyptians Abroad, known as *al-Rabitah*, which was founded by Munir himself in the early 1980s to be responsible for the affairs of Egyptian Brotherhood members outside their home country. Thousands of members who fled Egypt between the 1950s and 1980s found refuge in the Arab countries of the Gulf and, over the years, supported their organization at home with money and expertise. The association facilitated this support. Its mandate covered only the affairs of the Brotherhood diaspora and not those inside Egypt, but since Mohamed Morsi's ousting in 2013, the association started to make decisions on behalf of the imprisoned leaders in Egypt. In October and November 2013, the Association of Egyptians Abroad created central committees to activate anti-coup actions in the domains of media, politics, law, and human rights.[7]

According to an internal Brotherhood document that we obtained, around the time of the 2013 military coup, the Brotherhood's leadership anticipated future hardships and delegated four of its members to leave the country to represent the movement abroad and to support its activities in Egypt. The four were Mahmoud Ezzat, who rejected the assignment; Mohiye Hamed, a member of the Guidance Bureau and the contact point between the bureau and the presidency during Morsi's tenure; Gomaa Amin, a deputy to the general guide and the Brotherhood's historian for many years; and Mahmoud Hussein, the Brotherhood's secretary-general since 2009, who was already abroad at the time of the coup for personal reasons. Hussein's position as secretary-general would later be one of the main sources of conflict that led to a major split between the HAC and the historical leadership of the Brotherhood.

The High Administrative Committee

Since its inception, the HAC had to answer the question of its legitimacy as a substitute for the Guidance Bureau. This is why, under the leadership of Mohamed Taha Wahdan and then Mohamed Kamal, the HAC prioritized the restoration of the organization and bringing in new blood by including younger members in the leadership structure.[8] The HAC abolished several central committees while renaming and changing the mandate of others. For example, the Central Committee for Pre-University Students was annulled, while the Central Committee of Charity, that previously oversaw the dissemination of goods and services to the poor and disadvantaged in Egyptian society writ large, was changed to the Afflicted Committee and its work focused on the Brotherhood families of detainees and victims of the state's violence.[9]

The HAC also announced, in March 2014, a six-month-plan of protests and activities to increase the pressure on the regime and disseminate the Brotherhood narrative throughout society. The plan came in for harsh criticism from mid-level leaders and members alike for being "weak," "flawed," and "sluggish."[10] The Brotherhood wanted more. The plan changed nothing and the government stepped up its crackdown on Brotherhood members and supporters to unprecedented levels. The rising pressure along with the incompetence of the Brotherhood's plans led to a wave of malcontent among the group's base which began to object to the HAC leadership.[11]

Institutionalizing Violence

In the summer of 2014, in response to the state's violence and the anger of Brotherhood members, the HAC designed a three-stage plan that included an endorsement of "creative peacefulness" (*al-silmiyya al-mubdi'a*) or "qualitative operations" (*al-amaliyyat al-naw'iyya*), two terms that are used interchangeably and refer to the use of targeted violence against those confirmed to be implicated in killing or other grave abuses against Brotherhood members and supporters. Although some accounts suggest that there was general approval of these tactics within the Muslim Brotherhood, the subsequent internal conflicts indicate that the endorsement of armed struggle was far from unanimous and raised major concerns among Brotherhood leaders in Egypt and abroad. The HAC's plan came in conjunction with a significant rise in attacks against governmental buildings, electricity and telecommunication towers, and police personnel and checkpoints.

Since the military coup on July 3, 2013, Brotherhood protests were usually met with violence—whether from security forces or civil agents of the state. For instance, two weeks after the coup, thugs working in close coordination with security forces in Mansoura attacked a Brotherhood protest, killing four women, including a minor.[12] This attack and others like it led local Brotherhood organizers to arm several protesters at each protest with light firearms for defense purposes. Brotherhood protesters did not need central approval from the leadership to carry such weapons. However, over time, the arms became more sophisticated and lethal, and those who bore them started to use them in limited offensive attacks without the consent of the Brotherhood's leadership.[13]

The new controversial plan was supported by a slim majority of the HAC, but gained wider support among local leaders and heads of the administrative offices throughout Egypt. This was a clear indication that the radical changes within the movement were driven by mid-level leaders and the rank and file rather than the senior leadership.[14]

"You would be wrong to exclude personal and emotional factors in understanding the reasons some Brothers turned to violence," Ibrahim Munir, the eighty-five-year-old lawyer and acting general guide of the movement (2020–22) said in an interview with the authors. "These people saw their Brothers and Sisters getting killed in Rabaa. Their reaction has nothing to do with ideology or internal curricula."[15]

It may be true that emotions explain the initial outbursts of violence in the weeks and months that followed the dispersal of the sit-ins, but it does not explain the institutional decision that the HAC made about a year after the massacre. In fact, in the immediate aftermath of the massacre, Kamal and other leaders who would later come to form the HAC repeatedly rejected calls for retribution, and in September 2013 issued orders to ban all forms of armament at Brotherhood protests.[16] It would seem, then, that the HAC's decision to support violent activities against the regime came after long and careful reflection. Moreover, the HAC needed religious reasoning to provide grounds for its decision and counter the long-standing teachings of the movement. For decades, the Brotherhood had been asserting the peacefulness of the group's tools and methods and interpreting the teachings of Hassan al-Banna and the history of the group in the mildest of ways to sever any connection being drawn between the movement and political violence.

Banna's ideology, Badie's insistence on peacefulness during the Rabaa sit-in, long-standing tradition over the decades, the social fabric of the Brotherhood as mainly middle-class professionals, and its internal curricula—none of these gave grounds to support violence as a tool of political change. The advocates of political violence, however, found ways to reinterpret—or even twist—Banna's teachings and historical incidents in which Muslim Brotherhood members were involved in political assassinations. For example, Banna rejected the idea of revolution asserting that "the Muslim Brotherhood does not think about a revolution, does not rely on it, and does not trust its benefits and results," but in the same breath wrote that the "Muslim Brotherhood would use practical force if there is no other feasible way [to reform.]"[17] These statements are confusing, not only for an external observer, but also for members and supporters. Some people within the movement believe that the leadership had always concealed "dangerous" aspects of the Brotherhood's true ideology on topics like jihad, for fear that they would be abused, and that this concealed ideology might have provided grounds for effective resistance to the regime after 2013. In a 2018 phone interview, a former Brotherhood member in prison said that the Brotherhood youth in prisons had felt "betrayed" and "deceived" by the Brotherhood leaders for not providing them with a good understanding of resistance concepts like jihad.[18]

The HAC needed more well-grounded sources and reasoning to justify the use of violence away from the Brotherhood's ambivalent texts. The religious justifications the HAC were waiting for came in the form of two manifestos in January and May 2015. The first was an internal document entitled "The Jurisprudence of the Popular Resistance against the Coup," produced by a committee of Brotherhood scholars, formed by the HAC. It was the first Brotherhood document to call for resistance and the overthrow of the government using violent means.[19] In a letter that was made public months later, Mohamed Abdelrahman, a member of the Guidance Bureau who returned to activity in 2015 after many months in hiding, said that the document was not approved by the movement's leadership, a claim that Kamal rejected in another letter.[20]

The second document was a religious edict (fatwa) that bore the signatures of 150 Muslim scholars from twenty countries titled "Egypt's Call." The fatwa was seen by many as encouragement of the HAC's decision to use targeted violence against "perpetrators and those who incited against innocent souls," including "rulers, judges, officers, soldiers, religious scholars, media persons, and politicians."[21] The HAC hailed the statement as "the [true] religion" and the signatories as "the [true] clerics" of Islam.[22]

Just two days before the latter document was published, Mahmoud Ghozlan, a member of the Guidance Bureau, published an article on one of the Brotherhood's official websites asserting that "peacefulness" was the only way to resist the coup regime.[23] The article is believed to be written jointly with Abdelrahman al-Barr, another Guidance Bureau member who is known as the mufti of the Muslim Brotherhood. It called on Brotherhood youth and members "not to disbelieve in democracy," to continue the revolution, and "unite behind the idea of a free Egypt that includes all its citizens with no exception or exclusions." In the days that followed the publication of the article, government security forces arrested Ghozlan and Barr, as well as Taha Wahdan and Abdelazim al-Sharkawi, both Guidance Bureau members who were known for their disagreement with Kamal's positions in the HAC. The arrests indicated that at the very least the Egyptian government did not differentiate between those who called for armed resistance and those who advocated against it. Many are convinced, however, that the arrests took place as part of the authorities' continuing efforts to push opponents toward violent trajectories.

This orientation on the part of the regime was evident in several incidents that were documented in prisons. Mohamed Soltan, an Egyptian-American former political prisoner who went on hunger strike for 489 days before the Egyptian authorities released him on condition he give up his Egyptian citizenship, reported that prison authorities first sent him a prison imam to dissuade him from continuing the hunger strike. When that did not work, they sent Islamic State prisoners. He recalled:

> They started bringing in the ISIS guys. They would bring these guys because they were aligned with the authorities. They would

say that "only resistance is resistance. Everything else is futile; these people only respect the gun and power. They have no respect for the state of weakness you are in right now. You must have the strength to resist." [Radicalizing you through these tactics] makes perfect sense if the prison authorities can't convince you [that a hunger strike] is not religiously permissible (*haram*). It plays into their narrative if you decide to go the violent route.[24]

The Egyptian Brotherhood Abroad

Abroad, the situation for the Muslim Brotherhood was just as chaotic. After the massacre, thousands of Brotherhood members emigrated from Egypt in waves, mostly to Turkey, Qatar, Malaysia, Sudan, and a number of other African countries. Many of those who fled the country were among the most influential members of the group, some of whom had held ministerial and other official positions in Morsi's government, served as members of parliament, or were part of the second-tier leadership of the organization (such as General Shura Council members).

The presence of Egyptian Brotherhood members outside Egypt at this scale posed fresh challenges for the group's structures abroad. At this time, two entities directly led the Brotherhood's work abroad. The first was the Liaison Office of the Brotherhood Abroad, an entity founded shortly after the coup under the leadership of Mahmoud Hussein, the only high-ranking official who at the time of the coup was already out of Egypt on assignment for the Brotherhood and its secretary-general. Hussein traveled between several countries before settling in Qatar in 2013. Following regional pressure, Doha asked him along with several other Brotherhood leaders to leave the country in September 2014, and he moved to Istanbul, Turkey.[25] Hussein had institutional legitimacy as an elected member of the Guidance Bureau and had the connections that allowed him to be the focal point between Mahmoud Ezzat and the Brotherhood outside Egypt.

The second entity was the Association of the Muslim Brotherhood Abroad, the official representation of the Egyptian Brotherhood outside Egypt, which was managed by Mohammed Abdelwahab under the supervision of Ibrahim Munir, the founder of the association, as the secretary-general of the International Organization of the Muslim Brotherhood. The International Organization's role was mainly consultative in this period, trying to mediate between different factions.

The Liaison Office was not part of the Brotherhood's official structure, and so several Brotherhood leaders called for the establishment of an official body to represent the HAC abroad in the fall of 2014. At first, Hussein and Munir welcomed the idea.[26] This suggestion led to internal elections in the countries with the largest Egyptian Brotherhood presence in November and December 2014 to choose the members of the new envisioned body. The elections concluded with the formation of the Crisis Management Office Abroad (CMOA) with representatives from across the Brotherhood spectrum representing both the historical leadership and the HAC in Turkey, Sudan, Qatar, and Malaysia. The formation of the CMOA was announced in January 2015, and was led by Ahmed Abdelrahman, a medical doctor from Fayoum in Upper Egypt, who was directly appointed by the HAC. Abdelrahman was also a member of the General Shura Council, representing Upper Egypt, the same geographical sector represented by Kamal in the Guidance Bureau and where Kamal lived and worked. Another important development in January 2015 was the death of Gomaa Amin, the deputy chairman of the Brotherhood, in London, and the appointment of Ibrahim Munir as the new deputy chairman which made Munir the second-most senior leader in the Brotherhood.

Only days after the CMOA's announcement, the HAC, supported by the new elected leadership abroad, assumed control over the media outlets of the Brotherhood, including the official Arabic website, ikhwanonline.com. The HAC also announced the appointment of a new spokesperson under the alias of Mohammed Montasser.[27]

Montasser openly endorsed the "revolutionary option" on the Brotherhood's official platforms, and Abdelrahman made media statements in which he appeared militant. In April 2015, Abdelrahman appeared on Al Jazeera saying that the CMOA represented the Guidance Bureau in Egypt and that the Brotherhood had conducted a comprehensive review of its strategies and tactics. He said that the movement had conducted elections in the previous few weeks that changed 65–70 percent of the movement's leadership positions and that 90 percent of the current leadership was now young people.[28] Abdelrahman also asserted that the movement had concluded that "a reformist approach cannot work after revolutions," and that "radical change" is the only acceptable way forward.[29]

Hussein and Munir were angered by these statements and media appearances. The historical leadership of the Brotherhood, whether in Egypt or abroad saw an existential threat in the path being taken by the new leadership. Besides the "revolutionary option" that Abdelrahman and the HAC were advocating for, the historical leaders saw that Abelrahman was falsely implying that the HAC was replacing the Guidance Bureau and that it was not subordinate to it.[30]

Until then, the disagreements among the Brotherhood leadership might have been seen as growing pains that are natural during a time of upheaval. The developments that unfolded over the following month in May 2015, however, turned these disagreements into a legitimacy crisis by making them public to the broader Brotherhood base and the Egyptian public.

The Return of the Old Guard

Mahmoud Ezzat issued a statement in May 2015—the first since his disappearance in 2013—ordering the dissolution of the existing HAC and the establishment of a new HAC under the leadership of Mohamed Abdelrahman and with Kamal as a member. Ezzat also declared that the CMOA was to report to the Association of the Muslim Brotherhood Abroad in London under the leadership of Ibrahim Munir, effectively ending its subordination to the HAC inside Egypt.

In part, Ezzat's statement was a response to the HAC's support of the "revolutionary option." But other organizational considerations may have been more crucial motivations. The majority of the existing HAC members were in favor of amending the bylaws of the Muslim Brotherhood, which, if approved by the General Shura Council, meant that the group would have to immediately hold internal elections "from head to toe" and choose an entirely new leadership to replace, not only the leaders in prison, but also those in Egypt and abroad.[31] The mood of the movement's mid-level leadership and the internal constituents at the time—as shown by the most recent elections that had produced the HAC and the governorates' administrative offices—was in favor of Kamal and his ideas of change within the movement. In the Brotherhood's internal organization, the thirty-three administrative offices in Egypt comprise seven geographical sectors that cover the whole country. Following Ezzat's statement, only two sectors' representatives supported his decisions.[32] New elections in these circumstances would have meant that Ezzat would lose the position to which he had been appointed by Badie, which was unacceptable for him and his allies in the historical leadership in Istanbul (Hussein) and London (Munir).

For his part, Hussein issued a statement supporting Ezzat's decisions, confirming that Ezzat was the true leader of the movement, and not the HAC, and signed it using his old title: the secretary-general of the Muslim Brotherhood. The statement, as well as the use of this title, spurred an angry reaction from Montasser, the Brotherhood spokesperson, who said in a statement that Hussein had not been the secretary-general since the elections that the Brotherhood held in February 2014 in which it elected a new leadership and a new secretary-general.[33] Kamal also rejected Ezzat's decisions, along with five of the seven representatives of the country's geographical sectors. The CMOA rejected Ezzat's decisions as well, and announced that it would continue to report to the HAC and Kamal in Egypt. The HAC was never reconstituted according to Ezzat's orders. Kamal's control of the HAC was not to last, however.

On June 29, 2015, an explosion killed the Egyptian public prosecutor Hesham Barakat in Cairo.[34] Barakat was the highest-ranking official to be assassinated since 1990. Although no group claimed responsibility for the attack, the authorities accused the Muslim Brotherhood leaders of orchestrating the assassination. "The hand of justice is chained by laws," President Sisi said at Barakat's funeral, adding that "we will amend the laws to achieve swift justice." Clearly referring to imprisoned Brotherhood leaders, Sisi said, "they are giving the orders from their prison cells."[35] A day later, on July 1, Egyptian security forces arrested and then extrajudicially executed nine Brotherhood leaders in an apartment in Giza.[36] The victims were leaders of one of the geographical sectors supporting Kamal, and included Abdelfattah Ibrahim al-Sisi, the secretary-general of the HAC. The execution marked the beginning of a wave of similar incidents of extrajudicial killings that only intensified.

Old Is Gold (August 2015 to August 2020)

Following the killing of the Brotherhood leaders in Giza, most members of the HAC either went into hiding or fled the country. Ali Bateekh, for instance, realizing that his killing was imminent, boarded a plane to Turkey in the fall of 2015.[37] Magdy Abdelghafar was appointed as minister of interior in March 2015, and the authorities intensified their campaign of arrests and investigations to target those most active in the central committees of the Brotherhood.[38] Internally, Ezzat started to reactivate idle local leaders who had chosen to move to the margins in the aftermath of the coup and the massacre. The reemergence of these leaders tipped the scales in favor of Ezzat and the historical leadership of the organization.

One of the main tools that Ezzat's front used to curb members' enthusiasm for Kamal was to cut the financial support of the offices and geographical sectors that endorsed him. For decades, the Brotherhood's finances had relied heavily on membership fees and donations from supporters and sympathizers. The surplus of donations and membership fees were directed to fund businesses that loyal members ran and managed on behalf of the organization. These businesses were not confined to Egypt; the assets and companies of the Brotherhood are scattered in many countries in Europe, Asia, and Africa. Before the coup, it was the norm for the Brotherhood's branches and regions to provide for their own needs without central support from Cairo. This was the case for the student activities as well; Brotherhood students sponsored their regular events and activities without asking for central support. Local Brotherhood branches only occasionally needed the Guidance Bureau's support. Strategic events, such as elections, needed the central support of the Guidance Bureau and, in some cases, the support of members of the Muslim Brotherhood abroad.

Since the coup, and the subsequent arrests and closure of Brotherhood businesses, the members who worked and resided in rich Arab countries, East Asia, and Europe became the primary sponsors of the Brotherhood within Egypt. Most of these Egyptian Brotherhood members abroad had left decades earlier, and the Brotherhood branches in their respective countries had been led by the Association of the Muslim Brotherhood Abroad in London. Many of them had already developed personal relations with Munir and the other leaders of the association—an important aspect of the Brotherhood's financial affairs. This meant that the London office and the historical leadership—namely, Munir, Hussein, and Ezzat—had near-exclusive dominance of the financial routes and the funds supporting the local offices of the Brotherhood in Egypt.

The historical leadership used their newfound near-total control over Brotherhood finances to cut off support for their adversaries in the organization. This was effective in reining in Kamal, but had dire consequences for the trust between the Brotherhood's base and the leadership. Cutting off support affected not only the mid-level leaders in the administrative offices that supported Kamal, but also the benefits on which detainees and their families depended.

Low-level members and their families paid the heaviest toll. Many families of detainees in the administrative offices that supported Kamal and the HAC, such as in Alexandria, struggled to maintain a good standard of living, let alone support their loved ones in prisons. Stories of struggling families were posted online, and several went viral. Though many Brotherhood members, including senior officials, saw this exercise of control of the group's financial resources as a vile move by the historical leadership, the pressure from the families alongside other organizational and security-related factors effectively ended the support that Kamal's front enjoyed.

Between August and November 2015, the internal crisis only intensified. The Brotherhood appointed investigative commissions to look into the decisions and practices of Kamal's front; their findings were a full-blown condemnation of Kamal and his associates.[39] In September, several leaders who were linked to "qualitative operations" or "selective violence" resigned their posts in the Brotherhood and decided to work independently.[40] A second HAC was formed and attempted to distribute its roles and responsibilities between the Brotherhood's entities abroad (the association and the CMOA), but the association's leadership rejected the HAC's decisions. In November, the historical leadership held a meeting in Turkey and issued a statement to publicly denounce the violence that followed the 2013 military coup, implicitly accusing Kamal's faction of hijacking the movement by taking it into a violent direction.[41] The statement said that whoever proclaimed Brotherhood membership had to adhere to "absolute peacefulness" and those "who choose other ways are not from the movement, and the movement disavows them."[42]

Despite being true to the principles of the Muslim Brotherhood, the statement was misleading in identifying the "dispute over violence" as the main point of contention between the two rival fronts. It would be more accurate to say that the two Brotherhood fronts had, at the time, totally different—or even opposite—worldviews. They disagreed not only on how to oppose the regime, but also on the identity of the movement and its role in society.

Kamal's faction represented a revolutionary momentum that was keen to change the status quo as quickly and deeply as possible. In that sense, Kamal and his associates saw the movement as a means to an end: a revolution that would uproot the regime. In order to prepare the movement for this role, Kamal made many internal changes, including to the structure, bylaws, committees, and leadership, as well as reinterpreting the founder's legacy. In his famous quote, Banna rejected the whole idea of revolution, but the new leadership of the organization cast these comments as "historical" and "contextual," asserting that they "were not meant to be valid in all times and under all conditions."[43] Ahmed Abdelrahman, Kamal's representative abroad, accused those who claimed that Banna's ideas on revolution were among the Brotherhood's constant principles of "forgetting the fact that the movement already made up its mind to blend with the revolutionary status and moved toward this direction [during the January revolution.]"[44]

However, changing a movement as vast as the Brotherhood is not an easy task. The social fabric of the movement was formed around the idea of gradual change, and to alter this meant drastically disturbing the composition of the Brotherhood as a social group. Moreover, the historical leadership treated such ideas as an existential threat to the movement, which was not something that the elected leaders expected. As Yasser Fathy puts it: "The HAC was the de facto leadership of the Muslim Brotherhood, and because the movement was a centralized one, the HAC's leaders did not imagine that their decisions would be faced with such fierce rejection by the historical leaders."[45]

In that sense, the movement's old guard did not see the elections and the emergence of a new leadership as a sufficient reason to abandon what they considered to be the movement's core principles.

These historical leaders had long considered the organization of the Muslim Brotherhood as an end in itself. The effectiveness of the Brotherhood was not the issue for them, only its survival. Their orientation resembles the adage, "You have the watches, but we have time." This mentality was reflected in the leadership's decisions and statements. They appeared to be much more focused on the internal dynamics of the Brotherhood and how to maintain the hierarchy and the membership than on battling external challenges.

In an interview, a former political prisoner shared a conversation he had with Badie in 2014, when he was the general guide. The interviewee recalled Badie saying that the leadership would "stay in prison for ten, twenty years and then come back to power." This leadership, notably Ezzat and Munir, was imprisoned in the 1960s and saw the horrors of Gamal Abdel Nasser's prisons, but also saw how the Brotherhood had survived, flourished, and triumphed to become a leading organization in the country. "I've lived through 1954 and heard Egypt's leaders saying that the Muslim Brotherhood is finished," Ibrahim Munir said in an interview with the authors. "If we lose a generation, another one will emerge."[46]

The success of the Muslim Brotherhood, as framed by leaders and members, was often far from political, but rather social. A former Brotherhood member whom we interviewed recalled a parable that was recounted at an organizational meeting. During the regime's crackdown in the late 1990s, a middle-ranking leader who was under arrest and investigation, found himself the subject of derision by a state security officer. "You've been doing this for over seventy years, and you've gained nothing. You've had no successes at all," the officer said. The Brotherhood member soon turned the tables on the investigator, "I don't think we've had *no* successes," he said. "Actually, you are one of them." Startled, the officer asked how this could be the case.

"Do you pray?" the Brotherhood member asked. "Of course, I do," the officer confirmed. "Do you have a copy of the Quran at home?" the Brotherhood member asked, and the answer was affirmative. "Does your wife wear the veil? And do you send your kids to institutions or schools where they memorize the Quran?" The questions ensued, and the officer's answers were all affirmative. "Well, in the 1960s, the officer who was in charge of my investigation didn't pray, took pride in his almost atheistic convictions, and was married to a belly dancer, the Brotherhood member said. "As you can see, we've changed the face of this society, and you yourself testify to that."[47]

The former member, who had been ecstatic when he first heard this anecdote in the early 2000s, recalled how it later became problematic for him to believe it at all. In fact, it came to epitomize everything he thought was wrong with the organization: The Brotherhood had nothing in its possession to resist oppression and confront the regime. If the degree of repression has not changed, and only the lifestyles of those in charge shifted to be more religious, then the Brotherhood has changed nothing in the political equation. Even worse, if the Brotherhood's brand of religiosity is so devoid of any political content or ideology, to the extent that it could be embraced by the regime's own men without changing their heart about what they do to serve the regime and oppress the opposition, then the Brotherhood is indeed in a catastrophic position. The officer's remarks in the 1990s, in one way or another, seem confirmed. The Brotherhood has had no "political" successes.[48] This was not clear to the Brotherhood leadership, and was one of the reasons why Brotherhood leaders, as well as members, were so taken aback by the popular support enjoyed by the coup in the summer of 2013.

The Battle Ends

Montasser, the Brotherhood spokesperson, said on the Brotherhood's official media platforms that the HAC rejected the old guard's statements on violence. But the real-life situation came to be settled in favor of the historical leadership in December 2015. On December 14, Ezzat dissolved the HAC a second time and appointed the same leader, Mohamed Abdelrahman, to form a new one. This HAC was thus reconstituted by February 2016 without the membership of Kamal, the secretary general, or five of Kamal's supporters who had been members in the previous HAC.[49] Simultaneously, the London office issued a statement sacking Montasser and appointing Talaat Fahmy as the Brotherhood spokesperson. Montasser rejected the decision and said that the true leadership of the Muslim Brotherhood was in Egypt. A few days later, on December 20, Ezzat dissolved the CMOA, while four of its members issued a statement announcing their resignation from the office in objection to "its noninstitutionalized work and the violations of the Brotherhood's bylaws and traditions."[50] Only eleven of the thirty-three administrative offices in Egypt rejected Ezzat's decisions, signaling the deterioration of Kamal's support.[51]

In the months that followed, there were several initiatives to reconcile the leaders, all without success.

In May 2016, Kamal announced his resignation from "all executive posts" in the Muslim Brotherhood and called on other leaders to follow suit and to transfer the leadership to new elected leaders.[52] Kamal's call fell on deaf ears and spurred the London office to dismiss the Brotherhood leaders abroad who supported him including members of the CMOA Ahmed Abdelrahman, and Amr Darrag and Yahya Hamed, both of whom had been ministers in Morsi's government.[53]

The historical leaders had tightened their grip over the movement. In October 2016, Egyptian state security forces extrajudicially executed Kamal, justifying their action by describing him as "the founder of the violent arm of the Muslim Brotherhood."[54] Kamal's base of supporters was also fragmented across Egypt. However, in December 2016, this base pulled together. It held internal elections and announced the formation of a new entity to replace the

108 | BROKEN BONDS

Guidance Bureau under the name of the General Bureau. Simultaneously, Montasser and the CMOA announced the suspension of their work, having refused to dissolve on Ezzat's orders. Within a few months, the General Bureau would form an entity for the Egyptian Brotherhood abroad under the leadership of Kamal's associate, Ali Bateekh.

Despite the lack of human and financial resources, the General Bureau continued to have a presence on the Internet and a working body that published several outputs to tackle different aspects of the Muslim Brotherhood's problems. This was evident in March 2017 when it published a twenty-eight-page document to assess "the Brotherhood's failures of the past," which was intended to help its members to "learn how to improve their policies in the future."[55] The General Bureau produced another document on June 29, 2019, shortly after Morsi's death (Morsi died in a courtroom, after six long years of total isolation in Egyptian prisons). This document introduced what the General Bureau called a "new strategy" and articulated a novel framework for the Brotherhood in Egypt.[56] The strategy included a number of idealistic ideas on the Brotherhood's work that the majority of its leaders or members could not readily accept. One of these ideas was remarkably that the Brotherhood would not run for political power again. It would work only as an organization in the "national mainstream" and would "support all patriotic parties whose principles intersect with those of the Brotherhood."[57]

The strategy did not gain much momentum, within or beyond the Brotherhood. Nevertheless, it is one of the few documents that date the milestones of the internal discussions around the Brotherhood's political thinking. The historical leadership, which have been in control of the movement since mid-2016, have failed to produce similar documents that provide a new understanding of the Brotherhood's work in Egypt or creative ways of dealing with the challenges facing the group.

While the conflicts within the Brotherhood settled in favor of the historical leadership, the arrest of Mahmoud Ezzat in late August 2020 opened a new, bitter chapter.

A Crack in the Old Wall (September 2020 to June 2022)

In September 2020, just days after the authorities arrested Ezzat, the acting general guide of the Muslim Brotherhood, the organization witnessed the beginning of the most disturbing conflict in its recent history. Until Ezzat's arrest, it seemed that the Brotherhood included two conflicting fronts. But it turned out that the historical leadership was far from united. The following account of the crisis has been collected through several interviews, a few confidential internal documents, and many news articles and secondary sources.

At the time of his arrest, Ezzat was the only member of the Guidance Bureau who had not been imprisoned, killed, or forced to leave Egypt. The only other non-imprisoned Guidance Bureau member was Mahmoud Hussein, who had been abroad since before the military coup of 2013. For years, Hussein had been controlling the communications with the Brotherhood leadership in Egypt, including Ezzat himself. This monopoly on communications not only angered Brotherhood members and leaders because of its lack of transparency but also raised questions about the credibility and integrity of Hussein as a courier of orders from the leadership to the Brotherhood around the world.

Ibrahim Munir, for example, alleged that Hussein repeatedly blocked messages from the general guide, Mohammed Badie, that were meant for him and the rest of the leaders.[58] On the basis of these accusations, Munir, as the highest-ranking Brotherhood official in Egypt and abroad, and the acting general guide from 2020 (until his death in November 2022), took two significant organizational decisions. First, in September 2020, he decided to form a seven-member committee to assist him in the management of the Brotherhood's affairs. This committee, for many, was seen to replace the Guidance Bureau, whose living members were all in prison, except for Hussein. Second, Munir abolished the position of secretary-general, which Hussein had held for the past eleven years. The rationale behind Munir's decision was that, according to the bylaws, this position's title is "secretary-general of the Guidance Bureau" and not "secretary-general of the Muslim Brotherhood," meaning that the presence of an active Guidance Bureau was a prerequisite for the position of secretary-general to exist.

Munir's decisions received wide support from Brotherhood members, including those in prison, the members of the General Shura Council most of whom were based in Turkey, and the representatives of the General Bureau, which saw in it an attempt to "unite the ranks" of the Brotherhood.[59] Hussein, unsurprisingly, along with a small group of his associates, was fiercely opposed. One of these associates was Mohammed Abdelwahab, the head of the Association of the Brotherhood Abroad, which had been responsible for the affairs of the Brotherhood outside Egypt for the previous four years or so. For the last three months of 2020, according to a mid-level leader, Hussein impeded the work of the seven-member committee and suggested the formation of a new body that would consist of twenty members to run the Brotherhood as a replacement to the Guidance Bureau.[60]

Although it was Hussein who suggested the formation of the new body—which indeed formed, and became known as "the commission"—he refrained from attending its meetings and sent a message saying that he was "abstaining from attendance, but not from membership." The commission was not able to properly communicate with the Muslim Brotherhood leadership in Egypt without Hussein, a fact that reflected how much power Hussein had during his time as secretary-general of the movement.

Abdelwahab also refused to deliver to the commission the files he had as the head of the Association of the Muslim Brotherhood

Abroad. These files included key information, data, and connections in relation to the Brotherhood's political, financial, and media work. The association's branches in various countries, including Turkey, also refused to cooperate with the new body.

In response to these developments, Munir decided to hold internal elections to elect a new General Shura Council that could produce another body to lead the Brotherhood. The call to elections was rejected by Hussein's group in Turkey, and in response Munir disbanded the Brotherhood's bodies in Turkey in July 2021.

The next few months witnessed further fragmentation within the group. An internal document shows that Hussein tried to mobilize members of the General Shura Council and the leaders in Istanbul to officially withdraw their confidence in Munir. One of these attempts took place in the summer of 2021, when, according to a mid-level leader, four of Hussein's associates invited around fifty Brotherhood leaders to an Istanbul hotel to convince them that Munir should be ousted.[61] Hussein later issued an internal decision, signing it with the title of secretary-general of the Muslim Brotherhood, to demote Munir by limiting his responsibilities to managing the Brotherhood abroad and not in Egypt. The crisis continued when Munir announced, in October 2021, the suspension of the membership of six senior Brotherhood leaders, including Hussein himself. Hussein then attempted, with limited success, to gather signatures from Brotherhood leaders and Shura Council members to sack Munir.

By the fall of 2021, most of the regional offices in various countries had already taken the side of Munir. So when Hussein responded to his suspension by relieving Munir from his post and disbanding the twenty-member commission that led the organization in Turkey and that he himself had spurred into existence, his directives were ignored.

In November and December 2021, Hussein's faction issued statements to form a new entity to replace the general guide, and to appoint as its head Mostafa Tolba, a physician who was an important figure in the Egyptian Brotherhood in Saudi Arabia. The choice of Tolba as one of the key figures in the financial structure of the Brotherhood was indicative of the nature of this round of in-fighting. Hussein, who was accused in 2018 by leaders and members alike of financial misconduct and mismanagement, is still trying at the time of writing in 2022, to keep tight control over the Brotherhood's leadership and its financial resources by different means including the expulsion of thirteen members of the General Shura Council (probably half of the council's membership abroad) who joined Munir's front.[62]

Naturally, Hussein rejected claims that he controlled the movement and declared in a video published in November 2021 that he had not been "assigned to any post in the movement since 2015," and that his "participation in Brotherhood operations was because of [his] position as secretary-general and a member of the Guidance Bureau.[63] Hussein also said that all his recent decisions were taken with the approval of the General Shura Council, the entity that Munir's faction deems defunct, as most of its members are either in jail or dead.

This latest split is different from previous splits within the Brotherhood leadership. In the 2014–16 Kamal-versus-Ezzat split, both leaders and their associates were fighting over ideas, the essence of the movement, and its role in society. Each faction had radically different views about how to oppose the regime, the idea of revolution, and the relationship to partners and rivals. During the interviews for this research, several members and former members of the Brotherhood expressed respect that Kamal resigned from his post, which to them indicated that his demands to reform the movement were genuine.

In contrast, the Hussein-versus-Munir split was not based on conflicting ideas and worldviews. Rather, it appeared to be about the power of controlling the organization. Leading the Muslim Brotherhood has many material and moral perks. The financial flow is not as important, at least for Munir's faction, whose leaders agreed among themselves not to fight Hussein over the finances, because such a fight could harm the most vulnerable members of the organization in Egypt. The leaders who opposed internal elections during the 2016 conflict with Kamal, and forced their ideas on the organization despite the legitimate leaders' different views, now cite the bylaws and stress the importance of due process. The origins of the Hussein–Munir split have to do with organizational roles and, to a lesser extent, the benefits that some leaders accrue from their posts as responsible for the Brotherhood's institutions and platforms.

By the beginning of 2022, Hussein's faction seemed to be in a very similar position to that of Kamal's faction during the 2014–16 crisis. At the time of writing in late 2022, Hussein enjoys the support of only a few senior leaders, while he maintains control over a number of organizational media outlets. Hussein still controls the Watan television station, Ikhwanonline.com, and other social media accounts. Most importantly, Hussein's faction continues to control much of the Muslim Brotherhood's financial resources, particularly the funds that are directed to support the Brotherhood in Egypt; Munir's faction does not want to fight this battle for the time being.[64] Munir, however, was able to reap the support of the vast majority of divisions and sectors within the Brotherhood, whether geographical or technical.

It is important to note that Munir's internal victory was secured by the support of a few historical leaders who enjoy the respect of Brotherhood members around the world. One of these is Mohammed Behiry, who was imprisoned with Ezzat and Munir in 1965. According to a mid-level Brotherhood leader, Behiry mobilized Muslim Brotherhood members in the Gulf countries behind Munir.[65] Mahmoud Hussein, meanwhile, joined the Muslim Brotherhood in the 1980s, which makes him less credible among Brotherhood members who feel that legitimacy comes in large part from having endured the ordeal of long years in Nasser's prisons. These leaders are still able to influence the Brotherhood's decisions, often to a greater extent than those who hold senior positions within the group. This fact poses a serious question regarding the role that imprisoned Brotherhood members are going to play in the future of the movement.

Ibrahim Munir died in London on November 4, 2022, a few hours after attending a meeting discussing solutions for the issues of political detainees and the Muslim Brotherhood in Egypt. Munir told Abdelrahman Ayyash in a second interview on July 25, 2022, that he had been thinking about who should succeed him, and he trusted that the Muslim Brotherhood would figure it out. On November 16, Mahmoud Hussein appointed himself interim general guide, relying on a provision in the bylaws that states that the eldest member of the Guidance Bureau who is not in prison would assume this responsibility. His faction is a minority faction and does not represent the organization at large. The fact is that, as of late November 2022, there were ongoing convenings and conversations among top-tier members about Munir's successor. While there may be some debate on many issues, one thing these members agree on is that the next general guide will not be Mahmoud Hussein.

Although, at the time of writing, we do not know who the new general guide might be, we can say that certain factors will be at play. First, the new guide will not be a member of the Guidance Bureau, which will be a precedent in the movement, second only to Hudaybi's appointment in 1951. Second, the new guide will probably be old enough, whether in age or through his time in the organization to assume seniority. Third, the new guide will probably be someone who has not been publicly implicated in the legitimacy crises since 2013.

In our interview with him months before his passing, Munir told us that the Muslim Brotherhood was not planning on participating in political competition anytime soon. He reiterated the same message in a Reuters interview months later.[66] If the movement's leaders do indeed think this way, then the new guide will probably be chosen for his organizational and spiritual attributes—qualities that would be helpful in reunifying the group. The issues that involve negotiations with the Egyptian government and the maintenance of the movement's international relations will be on his agenda, but he will not be the one to take care of them.

Although the crisis may be over, the specter of future crises hangs over the group unless radical institutional changes take place. As Essam Telima, a former Brotherhood leader, wrote in an article published in October 2021: "The crises of the Muslim Brotherhood were never related to persons, they are related to the lack of institutionalism ... the lack of financial transparency and accountability ... and the lack of literature and curricula that keep up with the unfolding challenges facing the group."[67]

3
The Membership Crisis

"The trauma I have from the Muslim Brotherhood in Sudan is worse than the trauma I have from the Sisi regime"
—Omar, a former youth member of the Brotherhood who fled to Sudan

"I left the Brotherhood because I grew certain that neither party [within the Brotherhood] would be able to see its core tenets through. I left the Brotherhood because I believed in their ideology"
—Mahmoud, former youth member of the Brotherhood who spent almost four years in prison

The Massacre and Exile

After a ten-day trip across the Egyptian desert in 2016, Omar, a youth member of the Brotherhood at the time, arrived in Sudan.[1] As the crackdowns by state security forces grew increasingly repressive, dissidents often went into hiding in Egypt or fled to Sudan. Omar was received by a number of Egyptian Brotherhood members who had started to organize ways of welcoming and hosting members fleeing Egypt. One of these people was Ismail, a more senior member than Omar who was appointed as the person "in charge of the apartment" where he was staying. One day, Ismail called for a meeting of everyone in the apartment conducting what Omar described as a "formal investigation" into who had added eggplant to a traditional meal, *maqlouba*, that one resident had volunteered to make. The residents were interrogated about the decision to add the eggplant. Ismail was trying to find out if it was intentional and whether they had prior knowledge that a member of the Brotherhood who was more senior than them was visiting and disliked eggplant. If it was indeed intentional, this would be seen as typical of the disrespect that youth had toward elders in the organization.

Other similar investigations had taken place in the apartment. It was only a couple of weeks earlier that Ismail had launched another formal investigation, interrogating residents about body hair he had seen in a bathroom that was left uncleaned. Laughing, Omar recounted that Ismail tried to find the culprit by matching samples to suspects.

Recounting what happened, Omar remembered the horror of traveling through the desert and being smuggled across the border. He had spent years in hiding in Egypt after organizing and mobilizing people in the aftermath of 2013. The disconnect between what he had gone through and what Ismail was demanding of the residents spoke more to the lack of understanding of the severity of their plight than poor management. The pedagogical authority that more senior members typically have over younger members intersected with the organizational and logistical functions they were performing—in this case, managing an apartment. Ismail took this responsibility to embody more than logistics. These investigations were not simply investigations into the matter at hand; he was exercising his authority to interrogate the morals and motives behind actions. The maqlouba incident, the mystery of the bathroom body hair—these were moments of instruction. Throughout their stay, he would remind the residents of the good the Brotherhood had done for them in providing them free accommodation and meals. This exchange demanded complete loyalty, particularly at a time in which the organization was in crisis.

The membership crisis we posit that the Brotherhood ought to attend to is a manifestation of the legitimacy and identity crises discussed in the previous two chapters. In this transitional moment, much was lost in the attempt to maintain the sanctity of the organization and to cater to the needs of the Brothers and Sisters and their families. The lines between what was personal and what was political or organizational were blurred, and the most vulnerable often paid the price. The Brotherhood is dealing with a generation that has experienced an ordeal, as did the senior members, thereby challenging traditional claims of ordeal-base legitimacy. Further, a changing social and political context has rendered its traditional recruitment and retention mechanisms less effective. The experiences and challenges of the members themselves, across different countries, are now perhaps too disparate to be housed in the same tent.

This chapter is based on interviews with current and former members of the Brotherhood about their lived experience of being a Brother or Sister in the immediate aftermath of the Rabaa Massacre and after when they went into exile. It chronologically follows some of the most important moments that they point to in their lives within the organization. The chapter starts with the immediate aftermath of the Rabaa Massacre, before turning to some aspects of prison life and then life in Sudan and for exiles in general. The names and some identifying information about interviewees have been changed for security concerns. It should be noted that this chapter covers some of the same period discussed in the previous chapter during which significant structural changes and organizational developments were taking place; here the focus is on the experience of members.

Rabaa and Its Immediate Aftermath

In the months leading up to the Rabaa Massacre, activists and pundits had been calling for political reform, including early presidential elections or even the resignation of President Mohamed Morsi.[2] These calls culminated in protests in Tahrir Square on June 30, 2013. In response to these calls, the Muslim Brotherhood called for counter-protests and sit-ins that began on June 21. The largest of these was a sit-in at Rabaa al-Adawiya Square in the Nasr City neighborhood in eastern Cairo. By July 3, 2013, Abdel Fattah el-Sisi, who at the time was minister of defense, overthrew Morsi and his government, with the support of a coalition of civilian leaders.[3] In the months that followed, assaults by authorities against the protesters, many of whom were Brotherhood members, claimed dozens of lives.[4] As the summer dragged on, the sit-in resembled a site of resistance the state was not willing to positively engage. The steps Sisi took would come to resemble much of his tenure: a lack of civility in politics and an overestimation of what security crackdowns can achieve. The country was polarized, and Sisi was emboldened by a coalition of liberal, leftist, and Salafi forces to do what was necessary to initiate a new republic.[5] The state was also united in an effort to regain its standing after the scrutiny it came under during the 2011 revolution and its aftermath.

The scene at Rabaa was primed for the massacre. The thousands of protesters at the sit-in had been systemically dehumanized as "sheep" on public television and in other media, political parties were fed up with the Brotherhood, and Sisi had the support of regional allies to nip this project of political Islam in the bud.[6] Meanwhile, global allies including the United States refused to describe what happened as a coup.

On August 14, 2013 tanks rolled into Rabaa al-Adawiya Square.[7] Officers marched with their arms, snipers fired their bullets, and bulldozers tore down makeshift tents. In one incident, an interviewee described authorities shooting consistent fire above protesters' heads as they ducked in single-file leaving the sit-in. Ducking away from the bullets, one protester screamed a prayer to God: "Sufficient is God and he is the best disposer of affairs."[8] An officer ran closer, stuck a gun close to his chest, and yelled, "Do not pray for God to harm us. This is your fault. We are in the right. You are in the wrong." The officer used the gun to push the protester back into line. Avoiding the bullets inches away from his head, he marched out of the square.[9]

By the end of the day, at least 817 protesters were killed in Rabaa alone, according to a Human Rights Watch assessment.[10]

The regime stormed Rabaa with the intention to kill, on Sisi's orders. And while the largest number of killings in one place was in Rabaa, there were "mini Rabaas" throughout the country. Both military and police officers shot live ammunition at civilians. Makeshift hospitals were filled with injured and dead bodies. The final moments of Asmaa ElBeltagy, a seventeen-year-old girl and daughter of senior Brotherhood member Mohammed ElBaltagy—known in her life for being a budding intellectual, enthusiastic and contagiously joyful—were captured and posted online.[11] Dead bodies were burnt en masse by security officers.[12] People fleeing the scene were beaten, arrested, and disappeared. One photojournalist filmed the moments he was targeted and killed covering the crackdown on the frontlines.[13] The massacre was an exercise in nationalist fascistic prowess. It was a moment in which Sisi asserted his legitimacy to the public, and his then allies hedged their bets that he would become democratic after dealing with the immediate crisis. And listening to the statements of some of those members of the public who had wanted Rabaa to be dispersed, it could sometimes sound like they were endorsing a massacre to clear the square.

The final body count of August 14, 2013 is still contested, but it is clear that many hundreds of protesters were killed; Human Rights Watch conservatively estimates that about 1,150 pro-democracy protesters died in Cairo.[14]

The grim reality of the Rabaa Massacre and its precursor violence reflected what some young members had seen in the streets for months before. Mahmoud, a former member of the Brotherhood in his early thirties who was heavily involved in university student politics, said that in many ways he saw the massacre coming: "The decreasing popularity of the Brotherhood was inescapable. After winning almost all the seats of the student body in our university in the aftermath of the 2011 revolution and in 2012, we lost the presidency of the student committee. The parliament was later dissolved, the Brotherhood's popularity continued to decrease, and then we got to the June 30 moment."[15]

Mahmoud did not believe that the Rabaa sit-in would lead to meaningful change. After Sisi called on the public to give him a mandate to combat "potential terrorism," however, he could not conceive of staying home any longer.[16] As he left home to join the protests, his mother was wailing. "She knew I was not going to back down," Mahmoud said. "And we both knew that it was very possible that I would not return."

The Rabaa Massacre and subsequent arrests of Brotherhood leaders had a notable impact on the organization and its members. Many of our interviewees reported that there was a void in leadership: "The organization was in disarray," said Ayman, one of the members who was in crucial Brotherhood committees in exile. "This was different from waves of arrest under [Hosni] Mubarak. Back then, there was a ceiling on whom they would take. [Now] they took the first, second, and third tiers of the leadership."[17] This void resulted in a situation in which members, for the very first weeks at least, acted quite spontaneously. More importantly, the leadership vacuum left thousands of members whose friends and loved ones had just been killed with unresolved feelings and unrepresented grievances.

After Rabaa, the leadership and organization of protests were no longer centrally coordinated. This responsibility fell to the leadership of Brotherhood branches (*shu'ba*, plural *shu'aab*). "It fell on us to organize and coordinate movement and protest on the street," said Waleed, a member who was in the leadership of his shu'ba. He noted that in many ways, this was not initially difficult: "As a shu'ba, our day-to-day work is not that affected by the central leadership. About 90 percent of what we would do was a result of decisions we made and voted on."[18]

The security situation grew increasingly challenging. Waleed said that almost all Brothers left their homes in fear of arrests and reprisals. They moved to different parts of their city or even to other cities all together. Nonetheless, members found ways to coordinate and continue building momentum. Members relied on burner phones, and would text about protests within fifteen to twenty minutes of their start, or use funerals and more public settings to meet leaders and coordinate actions. The reality on the ground was bleak, and the challenges unprecedented. As we discuss below, some of the initial coping mechanisms (disassociation from central leadership, for instance) outlived their utility and came to contribute to larger organizational conflicts and crises.

The trauma of the violence and immense loss of the Rabaa Massacre deeply affected the lives of members. Some of our interviewees said that the echoes of men and women screaming still rang in their ears. The Brotherhood, at a communal level at least, is a very tight-knit organization. People who grow up in its communities, because of the level of persecution they have historically endured, can lead large portions of their lives engaging mostly with likeminded people. This is especially so in areas outside of Cairo and Alexandria. Security forces are much harsher and overbearing outside of the big cities, and there is less associational life, so the Brotherhood and the work one does for the organization—either in service of the members or the broader community—consumes one's life.[19] The vacuum left people who had either dedicated their lives and livelihood to the Brotherhood, or even joined at the height of its political success, with no answers and no immediate policy directions other than the general guide's words on July 5, 2013 in Rabaa: "Our peacefulness is stronger than bullets."[20]

Interviewees offered different accounts regarding whether official curricula taught in each usra were changed after the massacre, and whether the changes were meaningful. Some reported that the Brotherhood mandated that members memorize the Surah al-Furqan, a chapter in the Quran that discusses the difficulties Prophet Mohamed faced, alongside its exegesis. Others recalled that their weekly meetings were mostly delayed and consisted of check-ins and organizing work. A third set of interviews reported that there were discussions at their usra about what new or updated curricula should include. Some of the ideas floated included work on democratization in Latin America. These discussions, however, appear to have been ad hoc and location-specific. In our interviews with current senior leaders, they noted that official curricula were not updated at all, and that this was in fact a major organizational omission.

The vacuum bred confusion. Distraught over their loss, members' organizing and protesting became an act of exercising capacity in the absence of an overarching strategy. Members were concerned for the fate of the country, and were afraid of what was to come. Compounding the situation, the Brotherhood was on the verge of its first-ever vertical split. It was the first time since the early days of the Rabaa sit-in that members' lived experiences and organizational politics were publicly at odds. The split cut through countries, continents, and prison bars, and, in retrospect, was emblematic, laying the foundation for grievances that today remain unresolved.

After the Rabaa dispersal, the Brotherhood's leadership was effectively absent, while the streets were wholly mobilized. In many ways, this left the organization with the role of playing catch-up. Mobilizing in the aftermath of 2013 took many forms. People were still in the streets after the massacre, and they occupied the majority of the security forces' attention. The post-Rabaa protests were more an indicator of the larger discontent with the coup and its aftermath than they were evidence of any full-force mobilization by the organization. This was also reflected in the types of protests. One interviewee noted that one of the forms of protests "was known as *al-farasha* (the butterfly); just gathering all of a sudden for five minutes and dispersing," said Mohammed, a young protester who was actively involved in protests in the aftermath of Rabaa.[21] Another noted that sometimes the purpose of the protests was simply to show that the Brotherhood still existed. Mahmoud said that, in the first couple of years after Rabaa, the Brotherhood would organize flash mobs in city centers or, on occasion, set off fireworks. Even the full-fledged protests initially lacked strategic objectives. "We walked into the streets after the Rabaa dispersal, marched toward the city center, and did not know what to do next," said Omar, a member from Upper Egypt who was heavily involved in student activism. Omar added, "[T]here wasn't much of a plan at the time. People were just angry. I remember calling the senior leader responsible for our governorate, and he wasn't sure where to go afterward."

The months between August 2013 (when the massacre occurred) and October 2013 were crucial to the Brotherhood's development. Until October 2013, every administrative area within the Brotherhood organized its own activities and protests. The most senior leader outside of prison at the time was Mahmoud Ezzat, the deputy chairman of the Brotherhood. He was in hiding and had not given any directives for the organization, according to members we spoke with who were involved in decision-making processes. From October onward, and for a period of three months, a group of senior leaders within the Brotherhood, under the leadership of Mohamed Kamal, started organizing, creating committees, meeting, and strategizing about what to do amid the state crackdown. (Other aspects of this time period are discussed in the previous chapter.)

One of the hallmarks of Kamal's leadership was the emphasis on decentralization of decision-making. This iteration of the leadership, as noted in the previous chapter, was called the High Administrative Committee (HAC), which gave voice in the decision-making process to local and regional offices of the Brotherhood.

This contrasted sharply with how the rigid, heavily bureaucratic organization had previously operated. "This decentralization was paramount to how the Brotherhood was able to succeed at the time," said one member we interviewed who was active under the leadership of Kamal.[22] "The decisions went from a system of command-obedience to action within the realm of general guidance." Another member, Salah, who was involved and elected in his shu'ba, said that the emergence of this official leadership and the gap that arrests had created prompted elections in the early months of 2015 within every district to delineate the growing responsibilities the organization was facing.[23] These elections witnessed the rise in the ranks of some second-tier members—in other words, members who were younger and less institutionally advanced. Additionally, some senior members decided to sit the elections out.

Students, in particular, had to contend with this void of leadership in contrast to the Mubarak years when they had plenty of guidance. One of the leaders of student activism during Mubarak's regime, Hossam, described the structures under the Brotherhood at the time as very rigid. "It was hard for us to get much done without the approval of the higher-ups," he said. "The higher-ups were assigned, not elected. They mainly came from villages or provincial areas… and didn't have much experience dealing with people from different groups or parties. Whatever notion of a public sphere we had in Cairo, provincial areas lacked."

The security authorities' main challenge was dealing with the streets and protests organized in neighborhoods and other public locations. As one student leader put it, "We should have known that they were taking care of the streets before they gave us their undivided attention." But the reaction and activism of students would take on a life of its own when the school year resumed. And while students from Al-Azhar University in Cairo were brutally repressed, beaten, shot, and detained in the immediate aftermath of Rabaa, most universities around the country remained less hostile to the Brotherhood and student activism writ large. Student initiatives manifested as a myriad of organizations, both physical and virtual, under the banner Students Against the Coup. The main impact of these organizations and initiatives was to mobilize students. Initially, most student protests remained within the confines of their campuses. By the time students had sufficiently mobilized and security forces had sufficiently cleared the streets, the showdown between students and authorities grew to unprecedented heights.

Organizing in Crisis

After Rabaa, students continued to coordinate with more senior leaders, but the arrests and security concerns meant that they had leeway and autonomy. This is evident for instance in the caliber of students who took on leading roles in their colleges and universities. It manifested in what were essentially "crisis promotions" whereby junior students took on large organizational responsibilities and the hierarchical authorities grew thinner. These developments contributed to the citizenship problem within the Brotherhood. Among members, there is an unofficial bifurcation between people who were raised, tested, and tried in the organization from their neighborhoods and communities, and others who joined the organization at university. The long-term members are seen as more trustworthy, reliable, and dependable. The latter, however, are seen to be more "public sphere" folk, as one interviewee put it. University recruits "veer far from the source, from the core of the organization sometimes," one senior member of the Brotherhood remarked. "They are used to public declarations, big gestures, publicity. But this is not how we do things."[24]

But in the months after Rabaa, when centralized authority was lacking, members started acting hyper-locally, and at least for the first few months, there was apparently not much hostility between the youth and students, on the one hand, and elders and long-term members in their local communities, on the other. Initially, questions of violence and nonviolence were not fully systemized or organized among members. One interviewee described how rudimentary this process was at the start, noting that members would identify the homes of security officers and leave threatening messages on pieces of papers they slipped under their doors. The members would send these messages to officers who, they believed, were directly engaged in torture, ill-treatment of detainees, and, most importantly, gender-based violence against women. In particular, this mode of combating the targeting of women protesters was emblematic of what came to be known as "qualitative operations" or "selective violence" (discussed in the previous chapter).

Even as they had moved into their use of selective violence, Brotherhood members were still thinking of their actions on the spectrum of nonviolence. The slogan "Everything beyond blood is [considered] nonviolent" was frequently invoked.[25] This included some destruction of public facilities, but more importantly, it centered on protecting protests from state-sponsored violence. The theoretical justifications for this violence evolved, as did that of other, similar types of violence that grew out of the moment and took various forms. "Oftentimes the police would rely on street toughs to beat us up and throw us behind police lines," said Mahmoud. "I even met them in prison. They were afraid of us at first and apologized. I let them worry for a few days before I let it go."

The guerrilla-style violence of this period was both an outcome of the vacuum of Brotherhood authority and a response to the state's overreach. "What were we supposed to do, just let people, especially women, get beaten or arrested off the streets?" said one former protester, Salah. "Who was I going to go complain to or file a complaint with? There was no one." Brotherhood members walked on the far ends of protests with Molotov cocktails and handheld flares. Apart from protecting the protests, the overarching goal, as many interviewees reiterated, was "exhaustion and depletion" of police authorities.

"We knew, of course, that we did not have the capacity to mobilize against the military," Salah said. "As a matter of fact, our protests would go by some military camps, and we would leave them unharmed. All we wanted to do was provide protection for women, for protesters, and to make sure that we could say we were still able to mobilize protests on the streets." These efforts grew to be more targeted and aggressive. Officers whom they had identified as human rights abusers, particularly if they were believed to have been involved in torture or rape of detainees, were often beaten, or had their cars blown up.

It remains unclear how far these actions were conducted at the behest of the HAC. One of the members of the HAC, Alya, maintained that it "had called for ... 'creative nonviolence.' Under that banner, some members would oil certain streets so police cars and security forces would not be able to reach them, but there were never official orders to engage violently in a way that would harm people, including officers." This interviewee said that well-known attacks against officers during this period were in places where such actions would have happened without the Brotherhood's guidance or blessing. "A lot of these incidents were a manifestation of people's disappointment and disgruntlement," Alya said.

Other interviewees, however, maintained that the people who perpetrated these attacks had some guidance or at least coordination. They "did not operate on their own," Salah said. "Of course, there was coordination with their higher-ups." Another interviewee described a meeting attended by representatives of different colleges and rank-and-file Brotherhood members about responses to protests on university campuses. The discussions centered on the protection of protesters from the intensifying security crackdown and arrests. According to this interviewee, it was the college students who insisted on protecting the protesters using Molotov cocktails and other improvised weapons.

As noted above, the violence in the aftermath of Rabaa was not necessarily ideologically motivated. As the scholar Khalil al-Anani has noted, it is crucial to look into the agency and individual motivations of the people who perpetrated violence, and not simply consider their membership within the Brotherhood.[26] In his work on armed groups in the aftermath of the coup in Egypt, another scholar

Abdallah Hendawy notes that many of the people who went as far as to join organized, armed militias did so as an emotional response.[27] The notion that these acts were solely ideological does not allow for the wide variation among people who committed violent acts, the types of violence that was committed, or the views members took, including those who did not endorse any violence. In many ways, the explanation of violence among some Brothers post-Rabaa is not radicalization, but rather the lack of an overarching Brotherhood strategy.

Members, Leaders, and Security Forces

The reappearance of Mahmoud Ezzat in mid-2015 complicated the scene significantly. He had been in hiding, and low-ranking members had not only assumed responsibility, but gained notable popularity, particularly among the youth. These members maintained that they had taken on the brunt of the responsibility at a time when the most senior leadership was nowhere to be found. When a former senior member reappeared in the neighborhood and in committee meetings after hearing about Ezzat's return, Salah was unimpressed. "These people chose to stay at home when we were in the streets protesting," he said. "They told us not to talk to them, not to knock on their doors, and not even to approach them on the streets." Their reemergence, to members who had maintained mobilization and protests on the streets, reeked of a takeover. It was these dynamics that enabled a dividing line of grievances between those who had paid the price of mobilization when it was most risky and those who had not. The divide had cascading effects throughout the organization. It was not simply a generational divide, but a manifestation of the lack of uniting figures and strategies.

The youth and leadership from the General Bureau we interviewed both maintain that their efforts were purposely mischaracterized and misrepresented. "I have no doubt that there were spies among the leadership," Waleed, a Brotherhood member who held organizational responsibilities in a Cairene neighborhood, said. "Sure, there was serious disagreement and there were efforts for reconciliation, but the media leaks only exacerbated the issue." Others complained not only that the nature of the leadership conflict was mischaracterized, but also the actions of the General Bureau. "It was not only about violence," Mahmoud said of the General Bureau's efforts. "There was a whole manifesto and strategy for how to deal with the regime."

The question of violence and responsibility aside, many of our interviewees noted that some of the steps the General Bureau took were uncharacteristically progressive by the Brotherhood's standards. They were openly revolutionary, not reformist; they conducted internal reviews about the mistakes the Brotherhood had committed from 2011 onward; they assigned seats for women and youth in the Guidance Bureau; and they created committees that members felt were truly representative. Additionally, they supervised elections for senior-level positions under very harsh security conditions. Most importantly, these sympathetic members noted, they had a strategy on how to end the coup, or at least curb the crackdown. The elections, many of the people we interviewed felt, were actually representative.

The conflict and how it was managed spoke to much of what the Brotherhood continues to contend with today: competing legitimacies, the lack of coherent and consistent internal processes, and the contradiction of an organization that has the mechanisms of representation but builds its legitimacy on less than representative means. The Brotherhood is an organization that is not led by bylaws but by patriarchal authority, as Mohammad Affan has noted.[28] This means that historical leaders or figures within the organization are given a different weight than other members. Their opinions and the decisions they support or take are taken more seriously than those of people who may be higher in the organization's hierarchy. In the scheme of this internal conflict, the rift between both parties within the Brotherhood came to be about legitimacy, as the last chapter discussed in detail.

These contestations over legitimacy were apparent in how members spoke about their sacrifices. Members like Salah stressed that *they* had been the ones paying the price on the streets while others were in hiding. Beyond that, as a former member said in an interview, there is a generation of members whose association with the Brotherhood came primarily through protests and state violence.[29] The traditional leadership, which had emphasized the value of sacrifice and honored it in the organizational hierarchy, was faced with a generation that they had not really raised, but who had endured extreme levels of violence and sacrifice. "I was one of the last generation of people my age to have seen the Brotherhood for what it really is, before all of this [Rabaa and the aftermath] happened," Ayman said, who is in his mid-thirties, commenting on the generation of members who rose up the ranks after 2013.

Narratives of sacrifice in the Brotherhood conferred authority on those who had suffered—more so than official processes or the committees tasked with decision-making. This is part of why, later on, individuals whose membership was frozen or who were kicked out of the organization maintained that they were still Brothers, even if the organization didn't officially recognize them as such.

This conception of ordeal-based individual authority had downstream effects on the organization, which were exacerbated as the security situation grew increasingly complex and members went into exile. The processes of promotion in the Brotherhood are very rigorous, whether someone is matriculating from one level or tier to another, being given more trust, or otherwise tested. On the other hand, the ways in which people are delegitimized, discredited, and even demoted lacks rigor and is easily spread and solidified by incomplete narratives. Phrases like, "Our Brother has good intentions and capabilities, but he has just deviated from our path slightly," or "We have heard some things about our Brother, but it is unclear if they are true," are used to discredit people. This type of delegitimization is incredibly effective in the Brotherhood both for structural reasons related to how information travels in the organization, and because the organization is built on complete trust in one another's sincerity.

From the vantage point of many members, the rift of 2015 was more of a security threat than a takeover. Many of the members we spoke to pointed to an Al Jazeera Mubasher interview with Mohammed Sudan, a Brotherhood leader, as the moment when they felt they had become increasingly vulnerable and dispensable to the regime. According to these interviewees, in the interview that we were not able to locate online, Sudan smeared members who had been active since Rabaa (and at times had used the violent methods described above), asserting that they were not from the Brotherhood, and calling them "terrorists."

"I was in prison at the time and saw it coming," Mahmoud said. "That's when the regime started being much more aggressive and shooting people upon contact." There was a feeling among the members that one group of the Brotherhood was being framed by the other.

Senior Brotherhood leaders, for their part, believed they were reclaiming the organization. But for many of the youth, whether or not they had engaged in violence or just stood in protest, they felt they had been discredited and sold out by the organization. The Brotherhood dealt with them as one would remove "a cancerous tumor for the greater good,"[30] as one senior member said in an interview. One Brotherhood member recalled a meeting in which a senior leader said, "the Brotherhood will not leave anyone alone. We will take care of your family if you are martyred. We will take care of your family if you are arrested. No one will be left alone." The member smirked. "Obviously none of this was fulfilled."

An Organization Larger than the Sum of Some of Its Members?

The contest for control of the organization intensified. Some governorates and branches stood by Mohamed Kamal's faction, while others aligned themselves with Ezzat's faction. As the last chapter detailed, Ezzat had much better access to the Brotherhood's purse strings, and so the amount of money allocated to protests, media operations, and documentation of violations that Kamal's faction had been leading shrunk significantly. "We had to shut down many of the projects we had developed since 2013 due to funding," Alya said. Most importantly, Ezzat's faction withheld money designated for families of martyrs and detainees from governorates, branches, and families who stood with Kamal. "This money was not theirs for them to instrumentalize in this way," Alya said. "This was money people donated for the families, for their livelihoods," Alya added. In a rare moment of comic relief, one interviewee noted that in the middle of an anti-coup protest in a governorate that was barred from Ezzat's funds, a protester stood with a sign that read "I support Mahmoud Ezzat." The effects and feelings of betrayal these rifts had on people's lives are still felt today.

As with many other Brotherhood policies and strategies described in this book, some of what the organization and its members did during this period essentially came down to applying tools that had been built for a pre-2011 reality and that no longer suited the new context. For example, rank-and-file members did as they were told by their elders, something the Brotherhood had greatly emphasized and admired in the past. They partook in elections when asked, protested, helped in any way they could, using whatever skills they had as media personalities, strategists, or even lawyers. Now, however, they were dealing with an organization that was riven from the top down, and these members often ended up paying the price.

The rifts between the two camps seeped into prisons. As arrests among Kamal's faction intensified, Kamal-supporters became more prevalent in the prison population. One former detainee described the polarization in the prison cells: "Every group tried to recruit from incoming detainees. It was almost surreal. Both groups had their literature in prison. I remember someone sharing an MP3 player with me and we listened to some of Kamal's memoirs. The MP3s also had lectures describing what was happening and giving a religious basis to Kamal's moves. Books and pamphlets were also smuggled in as recruitment material," said Mahmoud, recalling elements of his prison experience.[31]

Despite Kamal's calls and attempts at reconciliation, his public demonization generally played to the favor of Ezzat's faction. Members of the Kamal-allied General Bureau claimed in interviews we conducted that Ezzat's faction refused multiple calls for reconciliation, elections, or even a meeting between Ezzat and Kamal. Kamal's killing in October of 2016 had a chilling effect among members. This came three months after other members from the office were killed in an apartment in the city of 6th of October, a suburb of Cairo. The demonization of Kamal and colleagues led some members to believe that, as Alya said, "Ezzat's faction [was a] partner in Kamal's killing." There was a feeling that members and leaders were sold out, and their deaths went unaccounted for. It was increasingly unclear whether the Kamal–Ezzat feud was an ideological rift or simply a conflict for power. The cost of all of this was bloodshed and the main winner was the regime.

Exile and the Afterlife

The crackdown led to mass exiles with members ending up in several different countries, in particular Sudan, Qatar, Turkey, and Malaysia. The Sudan trip was especially strenuous. Members who fled to Sudan endured horrific conditions, walking for days on end in the desert. Upon crossing borders, they would be settled within Brotherhood-sponsored housing units (as discussed above). Qatar and Turkey were common destinations, as these countries had had close affinities with Morsi. Their regional politics had hedged their bets on political Islam, which made their transition into host states smooth. Finally, Malaysia did not require visas for Egyptians, and Brotherhood members there facilitated easy residence.

Exiles and migrations, at this scale, were out of the norm for the Brotherhood. As an organization, the Brotherhood historically emphasized and provided a lot of cordiality, fraternity, and, most importantly, community. Prospects were recruited through group activities and very cordial check-ins.[32] Members met with other members from their neighborhood in weekly meetings, group activities, or public facing services. Members could meet afterward in larger settings that were also geographically bound. In addition to the religious texts, in these check-ins and weekly meetings, people shared life updates and discussed any major difficulties they faced. Repression and the constant threat of detainment contributed to a sense of a linked fate among members.

Some of our interviewees recalled how this sense of brotherhood manifested itself in the most difficult of situations. "We were at a protest and the person who was supposed to lead the chants did not show up," recalled Ayman, a former member of the Brotherhood.

> This was one of the biggest protests after Rabaa, so it was important that we got it right. As the main organizer of the protest, I decided to step in and chant instead. As I was going up on one of the Brother's shoulders to start the protest, another Brother, and one of my closest friends, pulled me down gently, put his arm on my mouth to indicate that this wasn't my role, and went up and chanted instead. Moments later, he was shot down by a sniper and died immediately. That could have been me.

What Ayman described was certainly a significant sacrifice, but it was one of many stories we heard. Ayman himself recalled how the doors of Brotherhood members' homes were always open to each other. A phone call that a Brother was traveling to another city for a brief stint, or a family was relocating was often more than enough to arrange for all sorts of accommodations, he said. These familial ties and bonds, some interviewees told us, were the beating heart of the organization.

But in exile, things were different. Fraternity turned into a politics of guest-hosting.[33] When Ayman arrived to Qatar in late 2013, he thought that members of the Brotherhood would have their arms and homes open to them. After all, they had just fled massacres and extreme violence. What he found, he said, was the opposite. He was not welcomed into anyone's home, but pushed to live in a very shabby room with another Brother he had traveled with where they slept on piles of newspapers. In the hot Doha summer, the room had no air conditioner, and just a small window that functioned as an entrance for mice. They were required to sit in weekly meetings with other Brothers who had arrived in Qatar at the same time. Members of the Brotherhood in Qatar were worried about getting implicated by this incoming wave: according to Ayman and Mohsen, who also fled to Qatar, the members who were in Qatar prior to the coup worried that engaging with the incoming group would prove to be a security risk. Ayman vowed to make sure that anyone who came from Egypt afterward never had the same experience. The heartbreak of unfulfilled fraternity that such experiences created continues to be a grievance within the organization.

Mohsen complained about the lack of infrastructure within the Brotherhood in Qatar, particularly with regard to enabling the incorporation of newcomers. Mohsen said that in Qatar he had proposed a number of business ideas, both to sustain the organization and to provide employment opportunities for incoming members to resettle.[34] But while members were initially enthusiastic, they ended up finding jobs that were unconnected to the Brotherhood. This was a small example of the Brotherhood not fulfilling its traditional role of providing economic security for members: it was becoming less central to their lives.

A senior member described the severe conditions the migrants endured by pointing to the lack of any systemic solutions to their situation. Leadership "would create some initiatives to get people involved and working, and then would withdraw support from them," he said. "It is as though they just wanted to keep some people busy and occupy their time."[35] The economic viability of Mohsen's business or how much the initiatives the senior leader spoke about would have borne fruit is beside the point—members developed deep grievances toward the leadership that spoke volumes when organizational crises surfaced.

Members who had spent time in Sudan described the horrendous treatment they experienced. One of them, Salah, recalled that senior Brotherhood members in Egypt had said they would be taken care of completely: "If you travel at any point, the Brotherhood will sponsor the rest of your education." Nothing like that happened, Salah said. In Sudan, some members, particularly those seen to be close to or affiliated with Kamal, were reminded almost daily that they were being sponsored by the other faction's money. "They would tell us, you are all living on our dime," said Omar, who also went to Sudan. "Just so you know and to get your act together." These Kamal-aligned members would protest that the money they were relying on did not belong to Ezzat's faction, which was simply a courier for funds that belonged to everyone, "but nothing would stop them," Salah said. In contrast, members who were aligned with Ezzat received perks, including better stipends, better jobs, scholarships, and access to universities.[36]

The marginalization of members from the General Bureau continued in their new places of residence. Some of the interviewees claimed that they were pushed to pledge their loyalty to Ezzat's faction, represented by the senior members in Sudan, in order to get better treatment. In some cases, the Brotherhood failed to provide housing to those with the "wrong" factional affiliation. A video surfaced online in 2017 of a group of youth who were kicked out of the apartment they were staying in (the video has since been removed). After multiple requests to evacuate the apartment, a member closely affiliated with the General Bureau refused to leave. Members more closely affiliated with the old guard were relocated to another apartment. This left the General Bureau members to contend with the landlord, and Sudanese police threatened to forcefully evict them. The video, titled "They Kicked Out the Exiled" (*Taradou al-mutareed*) was spread by a semi-anonymous account and went on to garner millions of views. Egyptian media outlets used the video to propagate the message that the Brotherhood was selling out its own people. At least one person we spoke with refused multiple interview requests from some of these outlets.

These incidents and the discourse of grievance that rose up around them indicated the Brotherhood's inability to continue to speak to its own public. The General Bureau maintained what someone close to the issue described as a "sizable" office in Sudan.[37] The Sudan office had elections and the candidate who won, Ahmed Abdelrahman, demanded that members reveal their points of contact in Egypt. (One of the big points of contention between Mahmoud Hussein and Ibrahim Munir was exiled members' access to contacts on the "inside"—in Egypt.) They refused, thereby driving a larger wedge in the Sudan office. Many of the members who left Egypt had seen much strife and stints in prison, or shouldered large organizational responsibilities. In their host states, however, the Brotherhood struggled with how to manage members with such experiences. First, there weren't enough activities and ways to make sure everyone felt appreciated and honored for their expertise. Second, the accreditation of these members' roles and ranking were often delayed. Yousuf, a senior member in Turkey, described an episode in 2015 in Turkey when such a delay occurred, and a large group of Brotherhood members arrived only to be sidelined.[38] In Sudan, we documented at least one instance in which a member's ranking was formally demoted. The implications of these problems with credentials are not merely ceremonial. To the member, such a demotion discredits their sacrifice and their investment in the organization. To the organization, it means that the scope of the member's involvement on certain issues is restricted. As Ezzat's faction ultimately forced the dissolution of the General Bureau, some memberships were frozen and other members were kicked out of the organization. This sometimes had ironic or contradictory outcomes. "You cannot freeze my membership since, as a woman, I am hierarchically not allowed to be a member anyways," said a woman supporting the General Bureau.[39] While she had no formal membership, she was informally senior-ranking and held a committee position. Her comment not only speaks to the structural sexism in the Brotherhood, but to a larger issue of ownership: whose organization is it, and what does it mean to be a *member*?

A Revival of the Brotherhood?

The ways in which members reached the decision to leave the Brotherhood speak to the variety of grievances they contended with. Among the youth, these stories and trajectories are particularly relevant. There is a cohort of members who rose in the ranks and joined the Brotherhood as college students and student activists. For many of these, the cost of their politicization was incredibly high. Oftentimes, these members were freshmen and sophomores in college when they had to begin spending years on the run in Egypt, separated from their families, universities, and communities. These young men saw their friends killed, maimed, or detained, lost siblings and parents in the diaspora or to prisons, and in the span of a couple of short years endured tremendous levels of trauma. The ideas that brought them to the movement themselves came to be contested in organizational politics to the point that it seemed like the only effective steps the organization took were against its own members.

140 | BROKEN BONDS

It is important to note that the decision to leave the Brotherhood is an extremely hard one.[40] For many, their relationship to the Brotherhood is the most meaningful in their lives. Mahmoud, a former detainee, said that he left the Brotherhood because neither faction within it embodied Banna's founding ideals. For him, the Brotherhood was "not *brotherhood* enough."

Ayman left the organization in the aftermath of the General Bureau's demise because of how Ezzat's faction had dealt with the other party. "I left and told them, whoever stays in this organization as long as Mahmoud Hussein is the leader is not only a witness to injustice, but an active accomplice and is unjust themselves," he said.

Ayman added that every initiative for reform was shut down by the higher-ups. He noted in our interview that they were not listened to or even consulted on major issues:

> Hussein decided to do nothing. He hindered all our efforts. Every time anything was going to be successful, they cut the funding. The Brotherhood stayed dormant for years in exile. He [Hussein] was worried that if we did anything public or meaningful, we would attract unnecessary attention. I couldn't justify this to myself. We did not leave our country to lead better lives here [Qatar]. We are not economic migrants. We left to resolve the situation in Egypt. We owe it to the people behind bars. How can I justify doing nothing with all the freedom I have in the world, when they have no freedom at all?

Others left the organization because they deemed it wholly ineffective. One of the very interesting trends is the number of people who decided to pursue studies in social sciences in the aftermath of the coup. The head of a newly formed organization in Turkey for Egyptians in exile who are studying social sciences estimates that around two hundred graduate and undergraduate students study social sciences. This is noteworthy given that in the past, the

Brotherhood has been criticized for its reliance mainly on members from the hard sciences for senior positions.[41]

The question of money looms significantly in some of the members' articulations of their grievances. One member who worked closely with the organization while in exile said that in the immediate aftermath of the coup, people would call members from the office in exile and ask how to donate large sums of money. The ways in which this money was spent, invested, or wasted, he said, remain unaccounted for. In early 2017, some news sites reported the loss of over 140 million riyal ($37 million) after a Yemeni businessman Abdelalim al-Shalafi, disappeared with money he had allegedly taken from Brotherhood members and other businessmen in Saudi Arabia for investments.[42] This story is particularly interesting because it speaks to the sums of money the Brotherhood deals with—$37 million is a sliver of their overall budget, and the lost money initially went unaccounted for.[43]

The grievances about money came to the surface when certain governorates and families were denied their stipends due to the internal fights between organizational factions. The closest thing the Brotherhood had to a public relations crisis came in 2019 when a voice note was circulated among Brotherhood members on WhatsApp that purportedly recorded a conversation between two Brotherhood leaders, Amir Bassam and Mohammed al-Desouky.[44] In the recording, Bassam complained to Desouky that Mahmoud Hussein, the Brotherhood secretary-general, had just spent hundreds of thousands of dollars that belonged to the organization to buy an estate and a private car for his son. At the time that the voice note circulated, exiled members of the Brotherhood in Turkey received just two hundred Turkish liras (less than $30) each month from the movement. Officially, the Brotherhood rejected Bassam's claims on the basis of technicalities, but Brotherhood members saw the recording as proof of their leadership's recklessness, if not corruption.[45]

It remains unclear if this incident was a result of malicious corruption or if some of the structural conditions within the organization simply facilitated confusion. After all, the Brotherhood does not save its assets in its organizational name, so it is plausible that a senior member would be holding money at any given time for the well-being and benefit of the organization. But it is also plausible that there could be nefarious activity. For our analysis, however, the primary concern is not whether or not the incident was a case of intentional corruption. What matters is that rank-and-file members, whether in Egypt or in exile, felt that they were at an economic disadvantage and that they suffered the brunt of the organization's hardships while those at the helm of the organization lived much more comfortable lives. Some of these members also felt that there were cases of corruption and misuse of funds.

Such grievances persist today. Some members believe, for example, that the process of seeking Turkish citizenship has been turned into a business by Brotherhood members with access to Turkish officials. Others look at the lifestyles of some of the senior members and their families and compare them to other members who struggle tremendously. "Do you know what it means that this person drives a BMW in Turkey? These things are much more expensive there," one member remarked, referring to a member who has such connections, and who had enjoyed a seemingly inexplicable improvement in lifestyle in exile.[46] The member in question had won internal elections within the Brotherhood and was charged with liaising with the Turkish government on getting nationalities for members. He later lost internal elections but kept these contacts for personal use.

"They're all one and the same," Mahmoud said, referring to the factions in the latest organizational rifts between Mahmoud Hussein and Ibrahim Munir. "I can sit down and draw out all the business networks and entanglements between each camp. It's all business and money."

Questions of theodicy loomed large in the aftermath of Rabaa.[47] Some members began to question how God could allow such horrific things to happen to them. Overall, God featured in some interviewees' stories more than others. While some had their faith challenged by the events of Rabaa, others spoke of their faith giving them endurance during periods of imprisonment, hiding, or in relation to travel bans. One member, who was on a travel ban for four years, said that she saw these tribulations as a practical test of faith. While detained, she would think of a certain Quranic verse or religious value to strengthen her relationship with God. She remembered seeing signs everywhere that helped her stay resilient. At one point, she recalled hearing a Quranic verse that gave her particular strength: "And seek help in patience and prayers; truly it is extremely heavy and hard except for sincere believers."[48] Another detainee remembered his time in prison as incredibly spiritual. He recalled in our interview, "I would not have been able to make it out without this level of spirituality and connection."[49]

Behind Bars or in Diaspora

Prison, in many ways, was a microcosm of some of the structural issues that limited the Brotherhood more broadly. In prison, a number of former detainees said, the Brotherhood would give news updates about what was going on in the country. Multiple people, who were detained in prisons in at least three governorates in the immediate aftermath of Rabaa when the streets were still mobilized, talked to the authors about how these news centers were essentially propaganda machines. If confronted about this, the Brotherhood members would respond that the news centers motivated detainees and kept their spirits up.

It is not immediately clear how much of their own Kool-Aid the organization drank. A former political prisoner shared that members of the Brotherhood told him that prior to their arrests and in their capacities as heads of programs, some of the reports they would write to their higher-ups inflated the levels of behavioral successes in their areas. These included the number of people who had gone through different curricula, for instance. Further, in our interviews about the early days of the 2011 revolution, we found that, without fail, every conversation between a member and a senior member contained faulty data on the part of the leadership. One student activist asked a member of the Brotherhood's Guidance Bureau for blankets and tents for people to spend the night in Tahrir Square. According to the student activist, the senior member replied that "our reports indicate that there are no more than two hundred people in the square, there is no point in doing this." At the time, this activist noted, there were thousands.[50]

Another member, Haitham, recalled an instance in prison: "One of the senior Brotherhood leaders in our prison pulled me aside after I had finished a visit with my father. I had argued with this leader that the news they shared with us in prison was incorrect, so he was keen to share the news I had just received in another makeshift meeting between the prison's most senior members. I stood there to share what I had but was quickly shunned away. 'This meeting is not for the likes of you,' they said." In other words, Haitham was excluded from the meeting simply because he was too junior within the organization—even though he was an expert on the subject matter under discussion. Haitham responded that they were all in prison, and that behind those bars, they were the same.[51]

The anecdote recalls a formula that a non-Brotherhood detainee once told the general guide while in court: inaccurate information plus incompetent people equal a bad decision; but accurate information plus competent people equal good decisions—and that this propaganda policy was counterintuitive.[52]

All these stories reveal an entity that continues to prioritize the organization over its members. While this order of priorities may have been acceptable or necessary at one point in the Brotherhood's history, amid the current freeze on matriculation within the organization, the organization's human resources are its most vital resource—and they are being neglected.

As the Brotherhood works to reconcile with its members, it must contend with serious challenges. In a private meeting organized in May 2022 by senior leaders to address some of members' concerns, one young attendee pushed back on the very idea of the meeting. "Where were you over the last eight years?" he said. "We left death and prisons and you were not there for us. No one asked about us or even cared to check in. Before you bring us back in and pontificate about how to address the larger public after this leadership crisis, you need to look inward. Apologize to your own members. Own up to your faults."[53]

This type of rhetoric was common among some of our interviewees. Such interviewees would not consider returning to the Brotherhood without serious apologies and revisions. Others remain content with an organization that they still consider to be beyond reproach. Responding to how the developments between Hussein and Munir have affected them, one member said that the conflict was incredibly confusing. "People who we trusted on either side come out and levy accusations about former colleagues of theirs that we could never have imagined members saying about each other," he explained. "Every figure is pushed to make a decision on where they stand, and youth like ourselves are caught in the cross-fire. The truth is lost."[54]

For current and former members of the Brotherhood, Munir's takeover had an array of implications. Even though Munir and Hussein were allied for most of the period since 2013, one member who is close to Munir's faction said that the Brotherhood was now at a moment of "re-charting our own history," when people will be heard and initiatives will be taken seriously.[55]

Another member, who had resigned from the organization in protest at Hussein's leadership, said he was cautiously optimistic. "I tried sending some ideas through and they took the initiatives seriously and studied them," he said. "I don't know how long this will last, but there is at least a change of pace."

But a third member said the constant infighting made her feel, for the first time in her life with the Brotherhood, as though the organization might no longer be essential. The Brotherhood could probably shut down, she said, and a new group pick up some of its ideas and move forward without its baggage. "For the first time, I feel as though I belong less to the organization (*al-jama'a*) and more to the brotherhood (*ikhwan*)," she said. It was something of a revelation: the fraternal bonds that kept Banna's most noble ideas alive and sustained generations of activists in the face of decades of repression could persist—without the organization's stifling hierarchy and pointless feuds. In fact, that organization itself might now be the biggest obstacle to *Muslim brotherhood* as a force for change in Egypt.

Epilogue: Unvanquished— But No Path to Victory

The Brotherhood today is not the organization that Hassan al-Banna established in the 1920s. It is also not the organization that successive Egyptian regimes, Ted Cruz, Saudi Arabia, or the United Arab Emirates appear to think it is. To understand the Muslim Brotherhood is to understand how an organization has both endured and changed through successive waves of repression, and how these have differently affected the institution and its members. These waves of repression have informed how the organization views itself, how it behaves, and how it recruits and retains members. The complexity of studying the organization, in many ways, speaks to the complexity of understanding authoritarian durability, political and social participation in autocratic contexts, and a form of postcolonial political agency that has been able to withstand decades of official scrutiny.

The Egyptian Brotherhood has navigated the lines between political engagement, social and moral reform, and religious proselytization. In Egypt, its activities spanned running for professional syndicates, providing course notes and summaries to university students at economical prices, providing for the poor, and weekly meetings with members in which they read religious texts for spiritual and social development. To be a member was to be enveloped in a life that was seemingly more active and meaningful than the average life available to most Egyptians.

It is an organization that in one way or another was part and parcel of every important historical event in the country's history over the past nine decades. It organized and fought in the 1948 war in Palestine, partnered with Nasser and his Free Officers to organize the 1952 coup, gave several of its members to the gallows, established sister organizations around the globe, and helped overthrow Mubarak's regime in 2011—before the Brotherhood itself was overthrown in 2013 after a year in power. To be a member is to be part of all of this.

The organization, however, grew very unevenly, which has contributed to what we have called an identity crisis. Whenever the state closed a door, the Brotherhood saw other organizations in society (universities and syndicates, among others) as a window. The organization's modus operandi was to react—and considering the array of constant challenges and threats it had to contend with, who could blame it? But this strategy, over the long run, prevented the Brotherhood from having a positive definition of itself or its goals. Even as the organization grew more entwined with Egyptian society, the prospects that its project could succeed grew increasingly delayed and even unlikely.

Worse, the Brotherhood as an organization is rarely self-aware about its failures. In some ways, it thinks of itself as existing outside the timescale of Egyptian politics. Engaging in political and non-political activities day-in and day-out, its arc goes beyond election cycles. Existing ahistorically in this sense means that what a political party would see as a moment of defeat, the Brotherhood may see as just a blip in their historic trajectory. This type of ideological thinking puts them in a world where the organization is often satisfied with mere survival, or with having a largely apolitical effect on the religiosity of Egyptian society. While the Brotherhood is undeniably a part of the daily politics of Egypt, it fundamentally measures itself against a standard of gradual religious reform toward an ideal that contemporary society is not ready for—but will be, the Brotherhood reassures itself, someday. The Brotherhood uses this utopian, someday ideal to paper over the resentment that its members feel at the failures of their everyday politics. One member remarked that, even when Morsi was in power, leaders would assuage members' criticisms by telling them that this was not the government that Banna called for or the Islamic government they would like to see.

The Brotherhood created a kind of loophole for itself by defining the organization somewhere between being a political and social entity. This loophole allows for continuous renegotiation of what politics and religion are, and what a member is or ought to be doing. This ambiguity has given rise to the type of politicking and pedagogy that sits at the intersection of competency and trust; between those who are most capable or experienced on a certain issue and those who can continue to represent and honor the *true* identity of the Brotherhood. Throughout the organization, the lines between the personal, organizational, national, and the ummah are blurred. The definition of the true nature of the organization—what it is, what its goals are, and how it works toward them—was never systematized or codified, and changed from one cohort of leaders to another. As success, progress, and competence grew nebulous, personalities came to dominate, and certain members became much more prominent even as the mission of the organization became vaguer.

The crisis of legitimacy, as we have shown in this book, is a consequence both of successive waves of repression and detainment by the state, and of the organization's adaptability. The organizational crises in the aftermath of 2013 shed light on some of these issues, as formal institutions that once mediated or streamlined these grievances ceased to exist in the same way. Legitimacy came to play a role not only in who formally represented the organization, but in what membership itself looked like. This was evident in how senior members built their legitimacy internally. In the 2021–22 crisis, for instance, Mahmoud Hussein built much of his authority on having contacts with senior members in Egypt. Under pressure, he refused to hand these contacts over to Ibrahim Munir, a member who was technically more senior than him.

Furthermore, in attempting to legitimize Munir as the de facto general guide after freezing the membership of Hussein, people around Munir spoke to the fact that he had spent more time in the organization than Hussein. Leaders' legitimacy in the Muslim Brotherhood has been based on several factors, including age and organizational seniority, the length of their imprisonment during crises, their participation in the revival of the organization in the 1970s and afterward, and their participation in internal electoral mechanisms. This sense of historical legitimacy was weaponized against people like Amr Darrag, who was not seen as having any legitimacy to strategize for the organization, despite having served in Morsi's government. The recent conflicts are changing how members think of their leaders' legitimacy. The issue of historical legitimacy emerges in conversations some youth have with elders when they refer to themselves as the 2013 generation—as opposed to the 1965 generation.

The challenges of being a member of the Brotherhood, especially in the aftermath of 2013, are hard to overstate. Members became accustomed to the possibility of violence: one told us that, due to the state crackdown on protests after Rabaa, he learned to differentiate between different bullet sounds and identify their lethality before he knew what the guns themselves looked like. The membership crisis is, in many ways, an extension of the identity and legitimacy crises. The organization has not been able to provide strategic direction to members whether politically or pedagogically. Younger and lower-ranking members have now been through just as many tribulations as the elders, rendering ordeal-based legitimacy less meaningful.

Operating as an organization under duress and in exile has also exacerbated the tensions within some of the organization's electoral mechanisms, and revealed how those mechanisms are not truly representative. Many former members we spoke with did not leave the organization due to the high cost, but because they felt that it was all for nothing. Some still believe in the ideology, but struggle with the organization. The grievances of families, senior members, and youth remain unresolved. The organization has a human resources problem. In the current environment, without true reckoning with these grievances, while other variations of politics that take Islam seriously may continue to exist, former members will happily do so outside the Brotherhood tent.

The Way Forward

The Brotherhood's reach into distant villages in Egypt and over eighty countries around the world creates a sense of invincibility within the organization. During the 2012 presidential elections, the Brotherhood had representatives in every electoral circuit throughout Egypt. Their presence allowed them to announce the results of the elections—Morsi's victory—with great precision, well before the Egyptian elections authority. The question remains, however, whether this sense of invincibility is more myth than reality. There is an adage that senior members used to tell youth: The Muslim Brotherhood will survive with or without you, it has a life of its own. One interviewee we spoke with said that she used to think of the Muslim Brotherhood as being like a moving train on train tracks, one is either on or off. Reality has tested these assumptions to a serious extent.

Since 2011, the organization has been more public, and perhaps more liberal as well, in kicking people out. A group of youth were publicly pushed out in 2011, a cohort of leadership were kicked out in 2016–17, some believe that the organization handed their own to Egyptian police in 2017 and that they bear responsibility for their consequential extrajudicial killings, and the highest leaders were kicked out in 2021. This does not account for cohorts of youth who left the movement in the aftermath of 2013. Very loyal members to the organization would note that these people were expelled for violating rules and procedures, or that they were not high-level members. The reality of the matter, however, is that the organization lacks institutional retention and conflict-resolution mechanisms. And while the Brotherhood may have had a life of its own without its members in Egypt, the question remains as to how viable this is in exile where their most valuable resource is people.

In some of our interviews with senior leaders, there is a sense in which they recognize that running for every office, particularly the presidency, was misguided. Ibrahim Munir, when he was the de facto general guide of the Muslim Brotherhood, said that the Brotherhood did not know they would be faced with such fierce resistance from the Egyptian deep state. Another member noted that the decision to run came at a time when the Brotherhood was keen to build state institutions. This pushed them to run for parliament, mobilize for the constitutional assembly, and run for president. By the time Morsi was in power, however, as the interviewee remarks—all the elected institutions were defunct. The Brotherhood felt the pressure of providing for a demanding public.

A former official in the Freedom and Justice Party—the Brotherhood's political arm—shared that in the weeks preceding the coup, they were discussing a number of programs including delivering bread to people and providing gas tanks.[1] She remarked that this was not the job of a political party, but it was what they had to do nonetheless. One of the more popular Brotherhood-assigned ministers was Bassem Ouda, the Minister of Supply and Internal Trade for six months during Morsi's year in power who is now detained in inhumane conditions without due process. Ouda's popularity was manifested in a picture of him hanging off a delivery truck delivering gas tanks. This was perceived as a success as he, and Brotherhood members, immediately stepped in to supply his ministry's services. The irony is that Ouda got this done with Brotherhood members, not the ministerial infrastructure. It is thus inaccurate to say that the state did not hinder the Muslim Brotherhood's leadership, and it was naive for the movement to assume that there would not be resistance. We should also note that other equally senior members said that overpromising and running for the presidency was ill-advised. The decision-making process itself was a manifestation of many of the issues the organization contended with at the time.

While this book focused on the Muslim Brotherhood during a particularly tumultuous period, it is not immediately obvious that the challenges they have faced are very different from those faced by the state itself or any of Egypt's social and political groups. It is also not immediately obvious that the Muslim Brotherhood was much less successful than any of these other social and political groups either. At the risk of oversimplifying, similar to how the Brotherhood coalesced with the military in 2011, almost every political coalition and group in Egypt did the same in 2013. Similar to how the Muslim Brotherhood struggled with establishing internal legitimacy and decision-making processes, Sisi's successive governments have not been any more successful. Sisi detained both Sami Anan, a former member of the Supreme Council of Armed Forces (SCAF), and Ahmed Shafiq, a high-ranking military general, former presidential candidate, and former prime minister. Sisi's coup-proofing measures are also quite extensive ranking from changing the vast majority of the members of SCAF, changing the law to necessitate presidential approvals for the Ministry of Defense, and assigning his family members some of the highest offices in the country. Mahmoud al-Sisi became prominent as an intelligence officer after his father became president. President Sisi's other son, Mostafa, is an officer in the General Oversight Authority, and Ahmed, President Sisi's brother, is a prominent judge responsible for tracking the finances of opposition groups, particularly the Muslim Brotherhood.

The evident lack of a coherent strategy in Egypt vis-a-vis both leadership and political dissent is not indicative of much of an outlook or overarching strategy beyond survival. This is obvious in what commentators have referred to as turf wars between security agencies. Statements by Kamal Abu Eita, member of the presidential pardon committee that was founded in the spring of 2022, for instance, indicated that certain agencies within the state are interested in seeing political prisoners released whereas others want to keep them all behind bars and even arrest some of the committee members.[2] These turf wars are also evident in the 2016 killing of Giulio Regeni, the Italian graduate student, according to reporting by *The New York Times*.[3] These coordination issues between security agencies have been shown to be coup-proofing methods and increase the intensity of violence—both of which are net positives for Sisi.[4]

One of the common themes in our interviews was this insistence on noting that the members of the Muslim Brotherhood are first and foremost Egyptian, and that whatever issues arise in the streets are mirrored and represented in the Brotherhood. This applies to junior and senior leaders alike. Just as some senior Brotherhood leaders believe that conspiracies were secretly plotting against them since 2011, Sisi openly says that 2011 was itself a conspiracy to undermine Egypt. And as Brotherhood officials publicly refuse to apologize for mistakes they may have made, Sisi demands that officials "do not ask him about human rights." Mahmoud Hussein reportedly refused to apologize for the Brotherhood's mistakes citing prophetic tradition (*Hadith*) where it is mentioned that people are rewarded for attempting to do the right thing—"Why would we apologize for something that God has rewarded us for," Hussein noted.[5] Sisi expressed a very similar sentiment: "If God was not on our side, we wouldn't have been able to sustain this."[6]

The ways in which the Brotherhood is almost ontologically connected to the Egyptian state are noteworthy. In the aftermath of Nasser's era, Sadat famously relied on the Brotherhood to mobilize against his political opponents. Under Mubarak, the Brotherhood bridged the gap between citizens and lack of some public services through their charitable work. In all of these eras, the Brotherhood navigated the line of what was politically possible. When there was little political progress to be made, it expanded horizontally and broadened the membership base. When political, public-facing work seemed possible, the organization partook in more forceful initiatives. The Brotherhood's perception of the extent of the state's repression shaped how they organized at any given time. This was also evident in early 2014 when the active leaders decided to decentralize a formerly very centralized and hierarchical organization. The decision-making process became so decentralized that officials we interviewed from different tiers had substantial differences in their directives.

The counterrevolution that spread throughout the region has contributed to norms of authoritarian learning among many Arab countries. Some of these norms included a toolkit of repression against the Muslim Brotherhood, but to a larger extent against political agency writ large. This is evident in the overt targeting and arrests of Brotherhood members in Saudi Arabia and the UAE, deportations from Kuwait, crackdowns in Tunisia, and so on. When asked what the most important success the Muslim Brotherhood has had since 2013, a senior member responded: not being listed as a terrorist organization by the British government. Most recently, the organization has had to contend with new geopolitical realities in which the Qatari government have, on more than one occasion, asked for senior members to leave the country and the Turkish government has shut down Brotherhood-owned television channels. The additional level of securitization on the global scale is detrimental for the Brotherhood. It is no coincidence that the most recent general guide was London-based and that the youth around him called for opening up to the global stage.

The new legitimacy the Muslim Brotherhood is trying to build needs to address its communication problem in relation to both internal and external stakeholders. In speaking about the post-2013 political scene, Ibrahim Munir noted in our interview with him that people, particularly youth, had just gone through something dramatic and heartbreaking; their loss was incalculable. While true, this discourse and organizational vacuum is more indicative of the fact that the organization was not able to reach its youth—not that they were necessarily heartbroken beyond repair. Externally, the relationships between the Brotherhood and many other political groups remain strained. Beyond rare personal relationships across the political spectrum, the Brotherhood remains untouchable vis-a-vis political discourse in Egypt and in exile. This is particularly concerning as it remains the largest social and political organization both domestically and internationally. As Elizabeth Nugent has so astutely noted, perceptions of the severity of repression and targeting that groups believe they have endured contribute to their isolation.[7] In that sense, the Egyptian government is still able to draw divisions between these groups by curating an image of a perfect victim that is *releasable* from prison or invited to national dialogue initiatives, and one that is shunned from both. The little leverage left for the opposition in exile may be their unity against the Sisi regime, but at this point, it seems far-fetched.

The Egyptian Muslim Brotherhood is not an organization whose fate will be resolved through security-oriented approaches. The Egyptian state as it sits today is not one that is representative of Egyptians or their dreams and ambitions. The organization that has always been able to capitalize on this, and will continue to do so, is the Muslim Brotherhood. Their political idealism and rhetoric have not been sufficiently tested to organically decrease their popularity. The infrastructure of the state has continued to enable conditions that allow its rhetoric to resonate. The Muslim Brotherhood's idealism will continue to capture the minds of the Egyptian people, but the group will never be able to develop political platforms without real openness on the part of the state. Simultaneously, the Brotherhood will keep getting more popular as long as it is not forced to face the music of the real world.

In Egypt, the Muslim Brotherhood will keep gaining popular power, because they are capitalizing on things that no other group has been able to do as effectively. First, the Muslim Brotherhood is building on religion and religious nostalgia, and this is a strategy that the state under Sisi has also employed. Second, the Brotherhood is building on the narrative of victimhood, and the inhumane treatment they are subjected to by the state increasingly supports this narrative among the widening circle of the state's economic and political victims. Lastly, the Muslim Brotherhood is building on the dreams of the middle class in Egypt to be relevant, heard, and supported. And in the absence of real civil society or the possibility of meaningful political participation that could attract the middle class, there will be no venue for many millions of Egyptians to practice political and social work other than joining the Muslim Brotherhood and its likes. There is no doubt that the way the state has been dealing with the Muslim Brotherhood has limited the Brotherhood's recruitment capabilities, but history suggests that the setback will be temporary. The reasons for the Brotherhood's popularity are intrinsic in the state's failures in dealing with society's problems, and the highly securitized approach cannot be maintained indefinitely. So when the state loosens its grip over Egypt's population, the school of thought that Hassan al-Banna founded and that is rooted in centuries of Islamic political thought, will find a new audience it knows how to address, and the same old foes it knows how to out-wait and will have perhaps learnt to better out-maneuver.

The Muslim Brotherhood is not an organization that will be arrested or exiled away. It is an organization with deep roots and influence in Egypt and beyond. Some of its ideas have grown bigger than the organization, and some of the organizational ties have outgrown ideological ones. Nonetheless, it is an organization in crisis and these crises are almost endemic to the Brotherhood's existence. If and when the organization returns to Egypt, it is conceivable that many of these dynamics will repeat themselves. We could expect some expulsions, the emergence of a new leadership and loyalists, and for the crises the book has discussed to be seen as assets for the Brotherhood to leverage and negotiate their positioning. We do believe, however, that when in full force, the Brotherhood is closer to the streets than the military state and other opposition groups, and that ninety-four years of persecution are yet to disentangle it from Egyptian society.

Notes

Prologue

1. Usra meetings are obligatory for each group of five or more members of the Muslim Brotherhood, and are a defining feature of the organization. These meetings, which aim to enhance fraternity among members, focus on religious socialization and indoctrination.

2. Hassan al-Banna, "Letter of the Fifth Conference" (in Arabic), Ikhwanwiki.com, 1939, https://www.ikhwanwiki.com/index.php?title=رسالة_المؤتمر_الخامس.

3. Hassan al-Banna, "Letter on Teachings" (in Arabic), Ikhwanwiki.com, date unknown (probably 1945–47), https://www.ikhwanwiki.com/index.php?title=رسالة_التعاليم.

4. The first protests calling for political reforms also occurred in 2004, after the Brotherhood published "The General Principles for Reform in Egypt." Although the document had a few interesting ideas—alongside many other ideas that were unsurprising—its content did not spur much debate in Egypt, let alone a response from the regime. See "The General Principles for Reform in Egypt" (in Arabic), Ikhwanwiki.com, Muslim Brotherhood, March 3, 2004, https://www.ikhwan.wiki/index.php?title=مبادرة_المرشد_العام_ل(الإخوان)_حول_المبادئ_العامة_للإصلاح_في_مصر.

5. "Rights Group: Egypt Executes 3 Islamists Tortured to Confess," Associated Press, February 8, 2019, https://apnews.com/article/middle-east-egypt-executions-muslim-brotherhood-human-rights-watch-9b8f9bc9acee4de7b5bc582926ef613c.

6. Simon Jeffery, "Hamas Celebrates Election Victory," *Guardian*, January 26, 2006, https://www.theguardian.com/world/2006/jan/26/israel1.

7. We use the term "Islamists" for the lack of a better term, and not because it holds explanatory value on its own. The term "Islamist," by definition, refers to a person who believes strongly in Islam, especially one who believes that Islam should influence political systems. The term does not distinguish between varying political parties that were absorbed into their countries' political systems (such as the Turkish Justice and Development Party or the Moroccan Justice and Development Party) and those who adopted a violent ideology that is antagonistic to both society and the state (such as al-Qaeda and the Islamic State). It is ironic that the

term "Islamist" has been used to describe not only groups with major ideological differences, but also warring groups, as was the case during the war in Syria. It also appears to be used to describe members of groups, rather than laypeople who may have the same beliefs but no organizational belonging.

8. Ahmed Abdelati, "A Message to the Bloggers of Banna's Followers" (in Arabic), Ikhwanonline.com, November 17, 2007, https://ikhwanonline.com/article/32163/البنا-تلاميذ-29%-المدونين-%28إلى-رسالة.

9. On Clark, see Kevin Baker, "Ramsey Clark: A Liberal Crusader Who Embraced the World's Bad Guys," *Politico*, December 27, 2021, https://www.politico.com/news/magazine/2021/12/27/2021-obituary-ramsey-clark-520597. On the trial, see "Egypt Bars Ex-U.S. Attorney General From Islamist Trial," Reuters, July 15, 2007, https://www.reuters.com/article/us-egypt-brotherhood-idUSL1521701120070715.

10. Amr Hamzawy and Nathan J. Brown, "The Draft Party Platform of the Egyptian Muslim Brotherhood: Foray into Political Integration or Retreat into Old Positions?," Carnegie Endowment for International Peace, the Carnegie Papers Middle East Series no. 89, January 2008, https://carnegieendowment.org/files/cp89_muslim_brothers_final.pdf.

11. "Revolution in Cairo: April 6 Youth Movement," PBS Frontline, February 2011, https://www.pbs.org/wgbh/pages/frontline/revolution-in-cairo/inside-april6-movement/.

12. Ahmed Ramadan, "Dr. Mahmoud Ezzat: The General Guide Has Clarified Our Position on the Strikes" (in Arabic), Ikhwanonline.com, April 5, 2008, https://www.ikhwanonline.com/article/36119.

13. See Asef Bayat, "What is Post-Islamism?," ISIM—Leiden University Scholarly Publications, 2005, https://scholarlypublications.universiteitleiden.nl/handle/1887/17030; Gilles Kepel, *Jihad: The Trail of Political Islam* (Cambridge, MA: Harvard University Press, 2002); and Olivier Roy, *The Failure of Political Islam* (Cambridge, MA: Harvard University Press, 1994). On non-movements, see Asef Bayat, *Life as Politics: How Ordinary People Change the Middle East* (Amsterdam: Amsterdam University Press, 2010).

Introduction

1. Mohammed Shereen Fahmy is a judge who became infamous for using terrorism laws to prosecute peaceful opponents. Human rights organizations have accused Fahmy of responsibility for the death of Mohamed Morsi in his court room in June 2019. Fahmy retired in June 2022. See "Egypt: Judge Mohammed Fahmy Punishes Dissidents with Endless Pretrial Detention," DAWN, October 1, 2020, https://dawnmena.org/judge-mohammed-sherin-fahmy; and "Egyptian Front Demands Discharging Judge Shereen Fahmy, Considering Him a Political Opponent Rather than a Judge as He Is Involved in the Slow Death of Mursi," Egyptian

Front for Human Rights, November 25, 2019, https://egyptianfront.org/2019/11/the-egytian-front-demands-discharging-judge-shereen-fahmy-considering-him-a-political-opponent-rather-than-a-judge-as-he-is-involved-in-the-slow-death-of-mursi/.

2. Ibrahim Munir (1937–2022) was an Egyptian lawyer and one of the most prominent Muslim Brotherhood members in the diaspora. He became the interim general guide of the Muslim Brotherhood after the arrest of Mahmoud Ezzat in August 2020 and served until his death in London on November 4, 2022. For more on Munir, see "Ibrahim Munir: Muslim Brotherhood's Acting Leader Dies in London," *Middle East Eye*, November 3, 2022, https://www.middleeasteye.net/news/egypt-ibrahim-munir-muslim-brotherhood-acting-leader-dies; and "Egypt's Muslim Brotherhood Rejects 'Struggle for Power,' Exiled Leader Says," Reuters, July 29, 2022, https://www.reuters.com/world/middle-east/egypts-muslim-brotherhood-rejects-struggle-power-exiled-leader-says-2022-07-29/.

3. *Quran*, 28:7.

4. Michael Schulson, "Why Do So Many Americans Believe That Islam Is a Political Ideology, Not a Religion?," *Washington Post*, February 3, 2017, https://www.washingtonpost.com/news/acts-of-faith/wp/2017/02/03/why-do-so-many-americans-believe-that-islam-is-a-political-ideology-not-a-religion/.

5. Hesham Gaafar, "Why Should We Free Ourselves from Studying Islamists?" (in Arabic), Al Jazeera, October 15, 2022, https://www.aljazeera.net/opinions/2022/10/15/لماذا-يجب-أن-نتحرر-من-الاهتمام.

6. David D. Kirkpatrick and Mark Mazzetti, "How 2 Gulf Monarchies Sought to Influence the White House," *New York Times*, March 31, 2018, https://www.nytimes.com/2018/03/21/us/politics/george-nader-elliott-broidy-uae-saudi-arabia-white-house-influence.html.

7. See Eric Trager, *Arab Fall: How the Muslim Brotherhood Won and Lost Egypt in 891 Days* (Washington, DC: Georgetown University Press, 2016); Samuel Tadros, Clifford D. May, and Johnathan Schanzer, "Fraternal Islamists: Getting to Know the Muslim Brotherhood," podcast Foundation for Defense of Democracies, July 1, 2019, https://www.fdd.org/analysis/2019/07/01/fraternal-islamists-getting-to-know-the-muslim-brotherhood/; Samuel Tadros, "Egypt: Security, Human Rights and Reform," written testimony for the U.S. House of Representatives Committee on Foreign Affairs Subcommittee on the Middle East and North Africa, July 24, 2018, https://docs.house.gov/meetings/FA/FA13/20180724/108598/HHRG-115-FA13-Wstate-TadrosS-20180724.pdf; Lorenzo Vidino, *The New Muslim Brotherhood in the West* (New York: Columbia University Press, 2010); Mokhtar Awad, "The Rise of the Violent Muslim Brotherhood," Hudson Institute, November 6, 2017, https://www.hudson.org/national-security-defense/the-rise-of-the-violent-muslim-brotherhood; Ed Husain, *The Islamist: Why I Joined Radical Islam in Britain, What I Saw inside and Why I Left*, (London: Penguin UK, 2015); Maajid Nawaz, *Radical: My Journey from Islamist Extremism to a Democratic Awakening* (New York: Random House, 2012); and Kepel, *Jihad*.

8. See Ioana Emy Matesan, *The Violence Pendulum: Tactical Change in Islamist Groups in Egypt and Indonesia* (Oxford: Oxford University Press, 2020); Marie Vannetzel, *The Muslim Brothers in Society: Everyday Politics, Social Action, and Islamism in Mubarak's Egypt* (Cairo: American University in Cairo Press, 2020); and Steven Brooke, *Winning Hearts and Votes: Social Services and the Islamist Political Advantage* (Ithaca: Cornell University Press, 2019).

9. See Hesham Gaafar, "Islamists and the Challenges of Building a Democratic Project," in *Islamists and Democrats* [*Islamiyyun wa dimoqratiyyun*], ed. Amr El-Shobaki. (Cairo: Al-Ahram Center for Strategic Studies, 2006); Ammar Fayed, "Is the Crackdown on the Muslim Brotherhood Pushing the Group Toward Violence?" in *Rethinking Political Islam*, ed. Shadi Hamid and William F. McCants (Oxford: Oxford University Press, 2017); and Mohammed Naeem, *Tarikh al-isamiya wal-garba'a: ta'ammulat naqdiyya fi al-ijtima' al-siyasi al-hadith*, [*The History of the Self-Made and Class-Hoppers: Critical Reflections on Modern Sociological History*] (Dar al-Mahrousa, 2021). Works by the other authors listed here are cited throughout our book.

10. Tarek al-Bishri, *Al-haraka al-siyasiyya fi misr (1945-1953)* [*The Political Movement in Egypt (1945-1953)*] (Cairo: Dar al-Shorouk, 2002).

11. Ibid., 33.

12. Ibid.

13. Salama Mousa, *Tarbiyat salama mousa* [*The Upbringing of Salama Mousa*], (Hindawi Foundation, 2014, originally published 1947), 33.

14. Mohammed Fareed, *Tarikh al-dawlah al-aliya al-uthmaniyya* [*The History of the Supreme Ottoman State*], (Hindawi Foundation, 2014, originally published 1893).

15. On Djibouti, see Abdullah al-Fateh, "The Islamic Movement in Djibouti, The Journey of the Summer and Fall" (in Arabic), Al Jazeera, April 28, 2017, https://www.aljazeera.net/blogs/2017/4/28/الحركة-الإسلامية-بجيبوتي-رحلة-الشتاء. On other countries, see "The Global Organization of the Muslim Brotherhood: Its Foundation and History" (in Arabic), Ikhwanwiki.com, https://www.ikhwanwiki.com/index.php?title=التنظيم_العالمي_للإخوان_المسلمين..._النشأة_والتاريخ.

16. "The Muslim Brotherhood and the Journey of the Movement: A Brief History of the Group and the General Guides" (in Arabic), Ikhwanwiki.com, https://www.ikhwanwiki.com/index.php?title=الإخوان_المسلمون_ورحلة_جماعة.»ملخص_لتاريخ_الجماعة_والمرشدين.

17. *Al-Natheer Magazine* 1 (in Arabic), May 29, 1938, Ikhwanwiki.com, https://www.ikhwanwiki.com/index.php?title=العدد_1_من_مجلة_النذير.

18. Ibid.

19. Hassan al-Banna. "Letter of the Fifth Conference" (in Arabic), Ikhwanwiki.com, https://www.ikhwanwiki.com/index.php?title=رسالة_المؤتمر_الخامس.

20. Ibid.

21. Khalil al-Anani, *Inside the Muslim Brotherhood: Religion, Identity, and Politics* (Oxford: Oxford University Press, 2016).

22. Ibid.

23. Hassan al-Banna, "Letter on Teachings" (in Arabic), Ikhwanwiki.com, https://www.ikhwanwiki.com/index.php?title=رسالة_التعاليم.

24. Hassan al-Banna. "Letter of the Sixth Conference" (in Arabic), Ikhwanwiki.com, https://www.ikhwanwiki.com/index.php?title=رسالة_المؤتمر_السادس.

25. This explication of the organizational structure is based on the authors' firsthand knowledge.

26. Salah Shadi, *Hasad al-'umr* [*The Harvest of a Lifetime: Pages from History*] (Cairo: Al-Zahraa for Arabic Media and Publishing, 1987), 27. The information in the following sections is primarily based on several memoirs and television interviews with leaders of the Muslim Brotherhood and the Special Apparatus, including, but not limited to, Fareed Abdelkhaleq, Salah Shadi, Ahmed Adel Kamal, Mahmoud Abdelhalim, Hassan al-Ashmawi, Mostafa Mashour, and Umar al-Tilmisani.

27. Ahmed Hamroush, *Thawrat 23 yulio* [*The Revolution of July 23*] (Cairo: The Egyptian General Book Authority, 1992).

28. Shadi, *The Harvest of a Lifetime*.

29. Ibid.

30. Ahmed Adel Kamal, *Al-neqat fawqa al-huroof* [*The Dots above Letters*] (Cairo: Al-Zahraa for Arabic Media, 1989).

31. Fareed Abdelkhaleq's interview with Ahmed Mansour, Al Jazeera, January 10, 2005, https://www.aljazeera.net/programs/centurywitness/2005/1/10/4-عبد-فريد-كم-يراهم-الإخوان-المسلمون.

32. Kamal, *Dots above Letters*, 221.

33. Yusuf al-Qaradawi, "The Muslim Brotherhood and Violence" (in Arabic), Ikhwanwiki.org, https://www.ikhwanwiki.com/index.php?title=الإخوان_والعنف.

34. "In Memory of the December '54 Executions, Hendawi Dwair, the Wronged Martyr" (in Arabic), Ikhwanwiki.com, https://ikhwanwiki.com/index.php?title=في_ذكرى_إعدامات_ديسمبر_54.._الشهيد_هنداوي_دوير_المفترى_عليه.

35. Ibid.

36. "Fareed Abdelkhaleq with Ahmed Mansour: The Shooting of Abdel Nasser in '54 and the Imprisonment of the Brotherhood" (in Arabic), uploaded to YouTube by Ahmed Mansour on September 15, 2020, https://www.youtube.com/watch?v=9ASzoPUduO0.

37. "The Muslim Brotherhood in Syria," Carnegie Middle East Center, https://carnegie-mec.org/syriaincrisis/?fa=48370&lang=en.

38. "The Muslim Brotherhood: The Muslim Brotherhood Around The World" (in Arabic), Ikhwanwiki.com, https://www.ikhwanwiki.com/index.php?title=الإخوان_المسلمون.

39. "Sayyid Qutb: The Martyr of Shadows" (in Arabic), Ikhwanonline.com, https://ikhwanonline.com/article/255401/1سيد-قطب-شهيد-الظلال.

40. Ibid.

41. Ahmed Abdelmageed, "How the 1965 Apparatus Was Formed" (in Arabic), Ikhwanwiki.com, https://www.ikhwanwiki.com/index.php?title=كيف_نشأ_تنظيم_1965.

42. Ibid. See also "Mr. Awad Abdelal, a Leader of the 1965 Organization and Talk about Memories" (in Arabic), uploaded to YouTube by aml2 aml2 on April 24, 2020, https://www.youtube.com/watch?v=wnovxJy8sCo.

43. Essam Tlima, "An Unpublished Document Tells the Story of the Apparatus of 1965" (in Arabic), Al Jazeera, July 29, 2022, https://mubasher.aljazeera.net/opinions/2022/7/29/-65#وثيقة-لم-تنشر-تحكي-تفاصيل-تنظيم.

44. Ibrahim al-Houdaiby, "Four Years Ago" (in Arabic), *Ibrahim's Blog*, January 8, 2008, https://ihoudaiby.blogspot.com/2008/01/blog-post.html.

45. YouTube, "Mr. Awad Abdelal, a Leader of the 1965 Organization."

46. This is contrary to Mokhtar Awad and Samuel Tadros's claim that "had it not been for an Islamist revival across Egyptian universities in the 1970s, the Brotherhood would have been history." See Awad and Tadros, "The Muslim Brotherhood: Terrorists or Not?" Hudson Institute, March 1, 2017, https://www.hudson.org/research/13398-the-muslim-brotherhood-terrorists-or-not.

47. This is a point made by the late Hassan Hathout, a very early Brotherhood member and one of the most prominent Brotherhood figures in the United States from the 1980s onward. See Abdullah al-Nafisi and Tawfiq al-Shawi, *Al-haraka al-islamiyya: ru'ya mustaqbaliyya, awraq fi al-naqd al-zhati* [*The Islamic Movement: A Futuristic Vision, Papers in Self Criticism*] (Cairo: Maktabat Madbuli, 1989), 73.

48. "The Interview of the Day: Why Did the Brotherhood General Guide Retire and Decide Not to Run Again?" (in Arabic), uploaded to YouTube by AlJazeera Channel on April 27, 2009, https://www.youtube.com/watch?v=IXNPZAiW6dY.

Chapter 1

1. Former member of the Muslim Brotherhood, interview with the authors via Zoom, March 2022.

2. For a discussion on essentialist literature on Islamism, see Anani, *Inside the Muslim Brotherhood*, 17, 22–25.

3. "Data for Egypt, Arab Rep., Lower Middle Income," World Bank, https://data.worldbank.org/?locations=EG-XN.

4. The "No" campaign was spearheaded by the National Association for Change led by Mohamed ElBaradei, and was made up of the Nasserist Dignity Party, the Wafd Party, the Coalition of the Youth of the Revolution, and smaller socialist and liberal factions, who all voiced their desire to see a new constitution. They made this call on the grounds of revolutionary ideas, mainly that the revolution had already brought down the regime and its constitution, so there was no point in amending it. Nevertheless, several figures associated with the "No" campaign also pushed for a "presidential council" to rule the country for an interim period, which was considered a rather undemocratic measure by Islamists, who persistently advocated for heading to the ballot boxes. See "Constitutional Amendments in Egypt between Supporters, Opponents and Reservations" (in

Arabic), Swissinfo.ch, March 17, 2011, https://www.swissinfo.ch/ara/29744746/التعديلات-الدستورية-بمصر-بين-المؤيدين-والرافضين-والمتحفظين.

5. Ali El Samman, *Documents of My Life, from the King to Nasser and Sadat* [*Awraq 'umri min al-malek ila abdel nasser wal sadat*] (Cairo: Al-Maktab al-Masry al-Hadith, 2005), 42.

6. M. H. Diab, *Intifadhat am thawarat fi tarikh misr al-hadith* [*Uprisings or Revolutions in Egypt's Modern History*] (Cairo: Dar al-Shorouk, 2011).

7. Ahmed Abdalla, *The Student Movement and National Politics in Egypt, 1923-1973* (Cairo: American University in Cairo Press, 1985), 26, 110.

8. Abdullah Al-Arian, *Answering the Call: Popular Islamic Activism in Sadat's Egypt* (Oxford: Oxford University Press, 2014), 109.

9. The Universities of Tanta and Mansoura in 1972, Zagazig in 1974, Helwan in 1975, and Minya and Minufiyya in 1976. They were established as expansions of departments formerly associated with Cairo University.

10. C. R. Wickham, *Mobilizing Islam: Religion, Activism, and Political Change in Egypt* (New York: Columbia University Press, 2003), 40.

11. Amir, interview with the authors via Zoom, 2022.

12. Qutbism had been discredited in 1969 by Hassan al-Hudaybi, Tilmisani's predecessor, leading some analysts to believe there was the possibility of an opening on the part of the regime toward nonviolent Islamists while Nasser was still in power. For a deeper discussion of Hudaybi's booklet against Qutbism in 1969, see Barbara Zollner, "Prison Talk: The Muslim Brotherhood's Internal Struggle during Gamal Abdel Nasser's Persecution, 1954 to 1971," *International Journal of Middle East Studies* 39, no. 3 (2007): 411–33.

13. Wickham, *Mobilizing Islam*, 91.

14. M. K. Al-Sayyid, "A Civil Society in Egypt?," *Middle East Journal* 47, no. 2 (1993): 228–42.

15. Wickham, *Mobilizing Islam*, 97.

16. Hesham Gaafar, "Islamists and the Challenges of Building a Democratic Project," in *Islamists and Democrats* [*Islamiyyun wa dimoqratiyyun*], ed. Amr El-Shobaki. (Cairo: Al-Ahram Center for Strategic Studies, 2006), 79.

17. Hadhoud, Mahmoud. "Neither Revolutionary nor Reformist.. The Ikhwani Ideology tested by the Revolution," in *Thawrat yanayer: qira'a naqdiyya* [*The January Revolution: A Critical Reading*], ed. Amr Abdelrahman (Cairo: Dar al-Marayah, 2019).

18. Joel Campagna, "From Accommodation to Confrontation: The Muslim Brotherhood in the Mubarak Years," *Journal of International Affairs* 50, no. 1 (1996): 294–95.

19. Ibid.

20. Omar Hussein, interview with the authors via Zoom, 2021.

21. The Brotherhood-affiliated television stations that launched in Istanbul after 2013 continue to be a subject of debate. For some, the oppositionist political message aired by these channels does have an impact on many Egyptians, despite

its low quality. As the argument goes, the Istanbul stations are no less professional than the regime's very own populist messages and commentators. Critics, however, believe that the political messages aired from Istanbul are only influential among marginalized segments whose impact at the political center is minimal, and that they lack the bare minimum of professionalism to create a larger and long-term impact. Comparisons are usually drawn here between the Brotherhood-affiliated media outlets and their Qatari counterparts, given the wide reach and impact of the latter.

22. "The Central Bank: The Rise of Egyptian Expats' Remittances to $31.5 Billion" (in Arabic), *Al-Youm Al-Sabe'*, March, 14, 2022, https://www.youm7.com/story/2022/3/14/5691050/البنك-المركزى-ارتفاع-تحويلات-المصريين-بالخارج-لـ5-31-مليار-دولار-خلال.

23. Nathan J. Brown, Shimaa Hatab, and Amr Adly, *Lumbering State, Restless Society: Egypt in the Modern Era* (New York: Columbia University Press, 2021), 140.

24. Mohamed Soliman, "Egypt's Informal Economy," *Journal of International Affairs* 73, no. 2 (2020), 187, 188.

25. Ibrahim Bayoumi Ghanem, *Al-fikr al-siyasi lil imam hassan al-banna* [*The Political Thought of Hassan al-Banna*] (Cairo: Madarat, 2012).

26. "In Numbers, We Publish the Results of the First Round of the Presidential Elections" (in Arabic), *Al-Youm Al-Sabe'*, May 28, 2012, https://www.youm7.com/story/2012/5/28/690592/بالأرقام-ننشر-نتائج-الجولة-الأولى-من-انتخابات-الرئاسة; and "Morsi Beats Shafik after Counting the Votes of the Voters in the Run-off in 37 Countries" (in Arabic), *Al-Masry al-Youm,* June 10, 2012, https://www.almasryalyoum.com/news/details/184994.

27. Affan, interview with Abdelrahman Ayyash, Istanbul, May 18 2022.

28. Hussein, interview.

29. Islam Lotfi, interview with the authors via Zoom, 2021.

30. Heba Ezzat, "Views on the Political Imagination of Islamists: Methodical and Political Questions," in Amr Al-Shobaki, ed., *Islamiyyun wa dimoqratiyyun* [*Islamists and Democrats*] (Cairo: Ahram Center for Strategic Studies, 2006), 17–62.

31. Nathan Brown and Amr Hamzawy, "The Egyptian Muslim Brotherhood, Islamist Participation in a Closing Political Environment," Carnegie Endowment for International Peace, Carnegie Papers, Carnegie Middle East Center no. 19, March 2010, 27, https://carnegieendowment.org/files/muslim_bros_participation.pdf.

32. Gaafar, "Islamists and the Challenges of Building a Democratic Project", 90; and Ezzat, "Views on the Political Imagination of Islamists," 32–34.

33. Abdel-Wahab El-Messiri, *Al-'almaniyya al-jiz'iyya wal 'almaniyya al-ahamila* [*Partial Secularism and Comprehensive Secularism*] (Cairo: Dar al-Shorouk, 2002).

34. Zeinab al-Baqari, "The Structures of Islamist Youth: Will It Become an Alternative to Large Organizations?" in Mostafa Abdel Zaher, ed., *What Is Political about Islam? [Ma al-siyasi fil islam?]* (Cairo: Marayah, 2018).

35. Amir, interview with authors via Zoom, 2022.

36. Ibid.

37. Baqari, "The Structures of Islamist Youth," 42.

NOTES | 167

38. Wael Gamal, "Lost Capital, The Egyptian Muslim Brotherhood's Neoliberal Transformation," Carnegie Middle East Center, 2019, https://carnegie-mec.org/2019/02/01/lost-capital-egyptian-muslim-brotherhood-s-neoliberal-transformation-pub-78271.

39. This account is based on that of Amir, a former Brotherhood member, interview with the authors via Zoom, 2022.

40. Bahey al-Din Hassan, "The Party Program of the Muslim Brotherhood in Egypt from a Human Rights Perspective" (in Arabic), Cairo Institute for Human Rights Studies, 2008, https://cihrs.org/برنامج-حزب-الإخوان-المسلمين-في-مصر-من/.

41. Amr Magdi, "Harsh Criticisms for the Draft Party Program of the Muslim Brotherhood in Egypt" (in Arabic), Al Jazeera, September 24, 2007, https://www.aljazeera.net/news/reportsandinterviews/2007/9/24/انتقادات-حادة-لمسودة-برنامج-حزب.

42. Brown, Hatab, and Adly, *Lumbering State*, 107.

43. Tim Eaton, "Egyptian Elections and the Muslim Brotherhood Bloggers versus Badei," *World Today*, 66, no. 11 (2010): 26–27.

44. Amir, interview.

45. Lotfi, interview.

46. Yasser Fathy, "The Muslim Brotherhood Youth: The Road to the 2012 Elections" (in Arabic), Egyptian Institute for Political and Social Studies, September 2019, https://eipss-eg.org/شباب-الإخوان-الطريق-نحو-انتخابات-2012/.

47. "Morsi: I Will Continue What Nasser Began to Build a National Industry" (in Arabic), *Al-Ahram*, May 2013, https://gate.ahram.org.eg/daily/News/806/25/207510/%E2%80%8F%E2%80%8Fالأولى/مرسي--ما-بدأه-سأكمل-عبدالناصر-لبناء-صناعة-وطنية.aspx.

48. Yolande Knell, "Egypt and Iran: Old Enemies Become New Friends?" BBC, August 24, 2012, https://www.bbc.com/news/world-middle-east-19347574.

49. "Egypt's Morsi Severs Ties with Syria, Warns of 'Counter-Revolution Violence,'" *Ahram Online*, June 15, 2013, https://english.ahram.org.eg/News/74082.aspx.

50. Ramy Nawwar, "Scholars of the Ummah at a Conference for Supporting Syria: Bashar al-Assad Is an Infidel" (in Arabic) *Al-Youm Al-Sabe'*, June 13, 2013, https://www.youm7.com/story/2013/6/13/1112776/علماء-الأمة-في-مؤتمر-لنصرة-سوريا-بشار-الأسد-كافر-محمد.

51. "Egypt's Brotherhood Refutes Saudi Fatwas Banning Support to Hezbollah" (in Arabic), Al Jazeera, July 28, 2006, https://1-a1072.azureedge.net/news/arabic/2006/7/28/إخوان-مصر-يرفضون-فتاوى-سعودية-تحظر-دعم.

52. "Egypt's Army Says Morsi Role at Syria Rally Seen as Turning Point," VOA News, July 2, 2013, https://www.voanews.com/a/egypt-army-says-morsi-role-at-syria-rally-seen-as-turning-point/1693911.html.

53. Mokhtar Awad and Mostafa Hashem, "Egypt's Escalating Islamist Insurgency," Carnegie Middle East Center, October 2014, 4–5, https://carnegieendowment.org/files/CMEC_58_Egypt_Awad_Hashem_final.pdf.

54. "The Islamic Forces Welcome to Erdogan Collides with His Talk about Implementing the 'Secular' Model" (in Arabic), *Asharq Al-Awsat*, September

15, 2011, https://archive.aawsat.com/details.asp?section=4&article=640456&issueno=11979#.YsckpP0zbIU.

55. Although Western observers are accustomed to the framing of Salafis as a regressive movement, the structural underpinnings of Salafism as a social movement appear to be intertwined with a partial eclipse of traditional clergy, which makes it at least partially a beneficiary of the social and political modernization of the post-1952 era, and not an antithesis to modernity per se, as some analyses propose. The Brotherhood school of thought, on the other hand, was inspired by the reformism of modernizing clerics—until its semi-Salafi turn in the 1990s. This makes it, as an interest group, closer to Al-Azhar as an institution.

56. One of the points of contention was Abd al-Ghafour's insistence on separating the religious and political arms of the movement—the Salafi Call and the Nour Party—and to brand the party in purely national terms as a party for "all Egyptians." Abd al-Ghafour, who spent the 2000s in Turkey, was probably influenced by the successful appropriation of party politics by Islamists and Sufis in Turkey since 1980, where he had seen how instrumental politics could be in protecting conservative interest groups, even in the absence of an agenda to transform the state. This prompted Stephanie Lacroix to brand the Nour Party a lobbying arm for a religious organization, rather than an Islamist party.

57. Stephanie Lacroix, "Egypt's Pragmatic Salafis: The Politics of Hizb al-Nour," Carnegie Endowment for International Peace, 2016, https://carnegieendowment.org/2016/11/01/egypt-s-pragmatic-salafis-politics-of-hizb-al-nour-pub-64902.

58. Lotfi, interview.

59. Amir, interview.

Chapter 2

1. Although many researchers have used the terms hawks and doves since the mid-1990s to describe conservative and pragmatic leaders respectively, the recent developments in the Muslim Brotherhood compel us to revise these terms. The fluctuation of many leaders between both sides, including Mahmoud Ezzat himself (who had been considered a Brotherhood hardliner but ended up endorsing more subtle and peaceful tactics post-2013) makes these terms irrelevant or outdated at best.

2. "The Spokesperson: Our Activities are Continuing Normally and Institutionally" (in Arabic), Ikhwanonline.com, August 28, 2020, https://ikhwanonline.com/article/241074/المتحدث-الإعلامي-أعمالنا-تسير-بصورة-طبيعية-ومؤسسية.

3. "The Muslim Brotherhood: From Inception until the Present Day," uploaded to YouTube by Foreign Policy Research Institute on November 2, 2013, https://www.youtube.com/watch?v=zRzlBbEg7I4.

4. Mohammad Affan, "Conference Proceeding: Going beyond the Exclusion-Radicalisation Premise in Understanding the Dynamics of the Muslim

Brotherhood Transformation after the 2013 Coup d'État in Egypt," *Rowaq Arabi*, September 23, 2020, https://rowaq.cihrs.org/conference-proceeding-going-beyond-the-exclusion-radicalisation-premise-in-understanding-the-dynamics-of-the-muslim-brotherhood-transformation-after-the-2013-coup-detat-in-egypt/?lang=en.

5. Victor J. Willi, *The Fourth Ordeal: A History of the Muslim Brotherhood in Egypt, 1968–2018* (Cambridge: Cambridge University Press, 2021).

6. "The Muslim Brotherhood: A Presence in 52 Countries" (in Arabic), Al Jazeera, March 21, 2016, https://mubasher.aljazeera.net/news/reports/2016/3/21/الإخوان-المسلمون-حضور-في-52-دولة/.

7. Ibrahim Munir, interview with Amr ElAfifi and Abdelrahman Ayyash via Zoom, April 30, 2022.

8. Affan, "Conference Proceeding: Going beyond the Exclusion-Radicalisation Premise."

9. Suhaib Abdelmaqsoud, the spokesperson of the Muslim Brotherhood, interview with Abdelrahman Ayyash, Istanbul, May 17, 2022.

10. Yasser Fathy, "The Muslim Brotherhood and the January Revolution" (in Arabic), Egyptian Institute for Studies, September 12, 2019, https://eipss-eg.org/الإخوان-المسلمون-وثورة-يناير--الجزء-الثالث/.

11. Affan, "Conference Proceeding: Going beyond the Exclusion-Radicalisation Premise."

12. "Update: 4 Women Dead in Mansoura Clashes," *Mada Masr*, July 19, 2013, https://www.madamasr.com/en/2013/07/19/news/u/update-4-women-dead-in-mansoura-clashes/.

13. Former Brotherhood member from Mansoura, interview with the authors, Istanbul, May 19, 2022.

14. Affan, "Conference Proceeding: Going beyond the Exclusion-Radicalisation Premise."

15. Munir, interview, April 30, 2022.

16. Fathy, "The Muslim Brotherhood and the January Revolution."

17. Banna, "Letter of the Fifth Conference."

18. Abdelrahman Ayyash, "Strong Organization, Weak Ideology: Muslim Brotherhood Trajectories in Egyptian Prisons since 2013," Arab Reform Initiative, April 29, 2019, https://www.arab-reform.net/publication/strong-organization-weak-ideology-muslim-brotherhood-trajectories-in-egyptian-prisons-since-2013/.

19. Affan, "Conference Proceeding: Going beyond the Exclusion-Radicalisation Premise."

20. Ammar Sharaf, "The Leadership Crisis inside the Muslim Brotherhood: Different Views and Lost Trust" (in Arabic), Ida2at.com, September 27, 2015, https://www.ida2at.com/أزمة-القيادة-داخل-الإخوان-المسلمين-وج/.

21. "150 Scholars from 20 Countries Issue 'Egypt Call' and an Edict on the Obligation to Stand against Sisi's Violations" (in Arabic), *New Khalij*, May 27, 2015, https://thenewkhalij.news/article/14781/150--الكائنة-نداء-يصدرون-دولة-20-من-عالما-ويفتون-بوجوب-التصدي-لانتهاكات-السيسي.

22. Mohamed Montasser (@montaseregy), the spokesperson of the Muslim Brotherhood, Twitter status update, May 27, 2015, https://twitter.com/montaseregy/status/603624269134823425.

23. Mahmoud Ghozlan, "On the Eighty-Seventh Anniversary of the Movement's Foundation: Our Call Remains, and Our Revolution Continues" (in Arabic), *Egypt Window*, May 22, 2015, https://old.egyptwindow.net/article/580417.

24. Walaa Quisay, "Carceral Fiqh and the Battle of the Empty Stomachs: Debates on the Permissibility of Hunger Strikes," unpublished paper.

25. Mahmoud Murad, "Update 4-Prominent Muslim Brotherhood Figures to Leave Qatar," Reuters, September 13, 2014, https://www.reuters.com/article/egypt-qatar-brotherhood-idUSL5N0RE05020140913.

26. Willi, *The Fourth Ordeal*.

27. "The Official Page for the Muslim Brotherhood Spokesman" (in Arabic), Facebook, https://www.facebook.com/M.B.SPOKESMAN1.

28. "The Future of the Struggle Between the Muslim Brotherhood and the Military and the Vision of the New [Brotherhood] Office Abroad with Ahmed Abdelrahman" (in Arabic), uploaded to YouTube by Aljazeera Channel on April 23, 2015, https://www.youtube.com/watch?v=Yey7EC8cCM8.

29. Ibid.

30. Willi, *The Fourth Ordeal*.

31. Fathy, "The Muslim Brotherhood and the January Revolution."

32. Ibid.

33. "The Muslim Brotherhood: Mahmoud Hussein Does Not Represent Us and We Will Continue The Revolutionary Path" (in Arabic), Al Jazeera, May 29, 2015, https://mubasher.aljazeera.net/news/miscellaneous/2015/5/29/الإخوان-محمود-حسين-لا-يمثلنا-وسنواصل.

34. "Egypt prosecutor Hisham Barakat Killed in Cairo Attack," BBC, June 29, 2015, https://www.bbc.com/news/world-middle-east-33308518.

35. "'Security Forces Dealt with Them': Suspicious Killings and Extrajudicial Executions by Egyptian Security Forces," Human Rights Watch, September 7, 2021, https://www.hrw.org/report/2021/09/07/security-forces-dealt-them/suspicious-killings-and-extrajudicial-executions.

36. "Egypt: Police Account of Deadly Raid in Question," Human Rights Watch press release, July 31, 2015, https://www.hrw.org/news/2015/07/31/egypt-police-account-deadly-raid-question.

37. Willi, *The Fourth Ordeal*.

38. Fathy, "The Muslim Brotherhood and January Revolution."

39. Willi, *The Fourth Ordeal*.

40. Affan, "Conference Proceeding: Going beyond the Exclusion-Radicalisation Premise."

41. "Egypt's Brotherhood: Our Peacefulness Is a Constant and We Will Not Deviate from It" (in Arabic), *Arabi 21*, November 18, 2015, https://arabi21.com/story/874035/إخوان-مصر-سلميتنا-من-ثوابتنا-ولن-نحيد-عنها.

42. Ibid.

43. Ahmed Abdelrahman, "The Muslim Brotherhood and the Revolutionary Status" (in Arabic), *Arabi 21*, August 16, 2015, https://arabi21.com/story/852175/الإخوان-والحالة-الثورية#author_1306.

44. Ibid.

45. Fathy, "The Muslim Brotherhood and the January Revolution."

46. Munir, interview, April 30, 2022.

47. Former member of the Brotherhood, interview with the authors, February 26, 2022.

48. Ibid.

49. Omar Owis, "Mahmoud Ezzat Announces The Formation of a New High Administrative Committee for The Muslim Brotherhood" (in Arabic), *Arabi 21*, February 15, 2016, https://arabi21.com/story/887978/محمود-عزت-يعلن-تشكيل-لجنة-إدارية-جديدة-للإخوان-المسلمين.

50. Omar Owis, "The Office of the Muslim Brotherhood Abroad Rejects Being Dissolved and Confirms the Continuity of Its Operations" (in Arabic), *Arabi 21*, December 22, 2015, https://arabi21.com/story/879108/مكتب-إخوان-مصر-بالخارج-يرفض-قرار-حله-ويؤكد-استمرار-عمله.

51. Ibid.

52. "The Speech of Dr. Mohamed Kamal, The Muslim Brotherhood Guidance Bureau Member" (in Arabic), uploaded to Soundcloud by Ekhwan online, May 10, 2016, https://soundcloud.com/user-906787785/pbpabknglzoa/s-m95EK.

53. Mohammed Khayyal, "Mahmoud Ezzat Freezes the Brotherhood Membership of Morsi's Ministers" (in Arabic), *Shorouk News*, May 19, 2016, https://www.shorouknews.com/news/view.aspx?cdate=19052016&id=19a75473-dfa8-49c1-8863-8d985c28b71d.

54. "Who Is Mohamed Kamal, the Muslim Brotherhood Leader That the Egyptian Police Killed?" (in Arabic), BBC Arabic, October 4, 2016, https://www.bbc.com/arabic/middleeast/2016/10/161004_mohamed_kamal_muslim_brother_profile.

55. Willi, *The Fourth Ordeal*.

56. "The Brotherhood's General Bureau Announces Its New Strategy" (in Arabic), *Arabi 21*, June 29, 2019, https://arabi21.com/story/1191180/الإخوان-المسلمون-المكتب-العام-يعلن-استراتيجيته-الجديدة.

57. Ibid.

58. "A Window on Egypt: A Special Interview with Ibrahim Munir on the Reality of the Disagreements between the Muslim Brotherhood Leaders" (in Arabic), uploaded to YouTube by Al Hiwar TV on October 15, 2021, https://www.youtube.com/watch?v=afGxZVWw208.

59. Taha al-Esawy, "Muslim Brotherhood Prisoners Appreciate [Munir's] Steps To Reunite the Group" (in Arabic), *Arabi21*, September 22, 2020, https://arabi21.com/story/1302158/سجناء-من-الإخوان-يثمنون-خطوات-لم-شمل-الجماعة-بمصر; Taha al-Esawy, "Egypt: The Muslim Brotherhood's Shura Council Approves Munir's Decisions and Here Are Its Most Significant Discussions" (in Arabic), *Arabi 21*, October 1, 2020,

https://arabi21.com/story/1304219/أبرز-وهذه-منير-قرارات-يقر-الإخوان-شورى-مصر
مناقشاته; Taha al-Esawy, "The General Office of the Muslim Brotherhood Welcomes the Calls to Reunite the Group" (in Arabic), *Arabi 21*, September 19, 2020, https://arabi21.com/story/1301426/الجماعة-شمل-لم-بدعوات-يرحب-مصر-لإخوان-العام-المكتب.

60. Brotherhood Shura Council member, interview with the authors via Zoom, February 22, 2022.

61. Ibid.

62. "Strong Organization, Weak Ideology; A Statement from the Muslim Brotherhood's General Shura Council," Ikhwanonline.com, July 12, 2022, https://ikhwanonline.com/article/254851/المسلمون-الإخوان-لجماعة-العام-الشورى-مجلس-من-بيان.

63. "The Comment of the Member of the Muslim Brotherhood's Guidance Bureau Dr. Mahmoud Hussein on the Recent Events" (in Arabic), uploaded to YouTube by the Muslim Brotherhood's account on November 25, 2021, https://www.youtube.com/watch?v=n-KcjkKqe54.

64. Mid-level leader, interview with the authors, Istanbul, Turkey, October 12, 2022.

65. Mid-level leader, interview with the authors, Istanbul, Turkey, July 19, 2022.

66. Dominic Evans, "Egypt's Muslim Brotherhood Rejects 'Struggle for Power,' Exiled Leader Says," Reuters, July 29, 2022, https://www.reuters.com/world/middle-east/egypts-muslim-brotherhood-rejects-struggle-power-exiled-leader-says-2022-07-29/.

67. Essam Talima, "Is the Muslim Brotherhood's Crisis Over?" (in Arabic), *Arabi 21*, October 21, 2021, https://arabi21.com/story/1392639/الإخوان-أزمة-انتهت-هل.

Chapter 3

1. Omar, interview with the authors, Malaysia, via Zoom May 22, 2022.

2. There is a larger story to be told about the involvement of the deep state and intelligence in coordinating some of these efforts. See David D. Kirkpatrick, *Into the Hands of the Soldiers: Freedom and Chaos in Egypt and the Middle East* (New York: Viking, 2018).

3. Kirkpatrick, *Into the Hands of the Soldiers*.

4. It is important to note that not all of the Rabaa protesters were Brotherhood members. There was a contingent of Rabaa protesters who were "with Rabaa but not with the podium," a group that believed that Morsi should not be overthrown by a coup, but also disagreed with the rhetoric and trajectory of the people manning the podium. There is also other context to the rhetoric espoused on the podium as different factions argued over messaging and strategy. It is crucial that the pro-democracy element of these protests not be lost on analysts due to their political biases. The banners on the podium and framing and messaging of Rabaa changed from being about supporting Morsi's legitimacy to supporting democracy.

5. Dalia F. Fahmy and Daanish Faruqi. *Egypt and the Contradictions of Liberalism: Illiberal Intelligentsia and the Future of Egyptian Democracy* (New York: Simon and Schuster, 2017).

6. May Darwich, "Creating the Enemy, Constructing the Threat: The Diffusion of Repression against the Muslim Brotherhood in the Middle East," *Democratization* 24, no. 7 (2017): 1289–1306.

7. "All According to Plan: The Rab'a Massacre and Mass Killings of Protesters in Egypt," Human Rights Watch, August 12, 2014, https://www.hrw.org/report/2014/08/12/all-according-plan/raba-massacre-and-mass-killings-protesters-egypt.

8. *Quran* 3: 173.

9. Rayan, interview with the authors, London, series of meetings March, April, May, 2022.

10. Human Rights Watch, "All According to Plan."

11. "Asmaa El Beltagy," uploaded to YouTube by SOS-Egypte Channel on September 26, 2013, https://www.youtube.com/watch?v=gKZs6AAKr2Y.

12. "Egypt's Darkest Day," Amnesty International, August 14, 2014, https://www.amnesty.org/en/latest/news/2014/08/egypt-s-darkest-day/.

13. Human Rights Watch, "All According to Plan."

14. Ibid.

15. Mahmoud, interviews with the authors, Doha, in a series of meetings, April and May, 2022.

16. Kareem Fahim and Mayy El Sheikh, "Egyptian General Calls for Mass Protests," *New York Times*, July 24, 2013, https://www.nytimes.com/2013/07/25/world/middleeast/egypt.html.

17. Ayman, interviews with the authors, Doha, a series of meetings, April 2022.

18. Waleed, interview with Amr ElAfifi, Dallas, Texas, August 2022.

19. Hossam, interview with the authors via Zoom, August 23, 2022.

20. "Muslim Brotherhood's Supreme Guide: Overthrowing Morsi Is an Illegitimate Military Coup and We Will Stay in Public Squares" (in Arabic), *Deutsche Welle*, July, 05, 2013, https://www.dw.com/ar/مرشد-الإخوان-عزل-مرسي-انقلاب-عسكري-باطل-وسنبقى-في-الميادين/a-16932560.

21. Mohammed, interview with the authors via Zoom, June 2022.

22. Alya, interview with the authors via Zoom, June 2022.

23. Salah, interview with the authors via Zoom, May 2022.

24. Tawfiq, interview with the authors, Dallas, April 2022.

25. Affan, "Conference Proceeding: Going beyond the Exclusion-Radicalisation Premise."

26. Khalil al-Anani, "Rethinking the Repression-Dissent Nexus: Assessing Egypt's Muslim Brotherhood's Response to Repression since the Coup of 2013," *Democratization* 26, no. 8 (November 17, 2019): 1329–41.

27. Abdallah Hendawy, *Bleeding Hearts: From Passionate Activism to Violent Insurgency in Egypt* (Lanham, Maryland: Lexington Books, 2021).

28. Affan, "Conference Proceeding: Going beyond the Exclusion-Radicalisation Premise."

29. Mohsen, interview with Amr ElAfifi, Doha, May 2022.

30. Mohsen, interview.

31. Mahmoud, interviews.

32. Anani, *Inside the Muslim Brotherhood*.

33. Lamis Abdelaaty, "Refugees and Guesthood in Turkey," *Journal of Refugee Studies* 34 no. 3 (2021): 2827–48.

34. Mohsen, interview.

35. Nabil, interview with the authors, Doha, April 2022.

36. Salah, interview.

37. Omar, interview.

38. Yousuf, interview with the authors via Zoom, March 22, 2022.

39. Alya, interview.

40. Mustafa Menshawy, *Leaving the Muslim Brotherhood: Self, Society and the State*, Middle East Today (Cham: Palgrave Macmillan, 2020).

41. Hossam Tamam, *Tahawwulat al-ikhwan al-muslimun: tafakkuk al-idiyolijiyya wa nihaya al-tanzim* [*Transformations of the Muslim Brotherhood: The Dissolution of Ideology and the End of the Organization*] (Cairo: Madbuli, 2006).

42. "Yemini Businessman Shalafi Disappears Amidst the Disappearance of the Muslim Brotherhood" (in Arabic), *Al-Arabi Al-Jadeed*, February, 18, 2017, https://www.alaraby.co.uk/"الإخوان-لـ-أموال-ضياع-وسط-يختفي-السلفي-اليمني-الأعمال-رجل".

43. Tawfiq, interview with the author, Dallas, April 2022.

44. "Amir Bassam, the Brotherhood Leader in Turkey, Exposes Mahmoud Hussein and Other Leaders in a Leaked Audio Message" (in Arabic), uploaded to YouTube by MBC Masr on July 26, 2019, https://www.youtube.com/watch?v=Oi31PHqEg6s.

45. See also Abdelrahman Ayyash, "The Turkish Future of Egypt's Muslim Brotherhood," The Century Foundation, August 17, 2020, https://tcf.org/content/report/turkish-future-egypts-muslim-brotherhood/.

46. Mohsen, interview.

47. Walaa Quisay, "Competing Theodicies: The Rabaa Massacre and the Problem of Suffering," *Political Theology* (April 7, 2022): 1–18.

48. *Quran*, 1:45.

49. Mahmoud, interviews.

50. Hossam, interview.

51. Haitham, interview with Amr ElAfifi, Doha, in-person, series of meetings in April and May, 2022.

52. Ibid.

53. Ayman, interviews.

54. Amal, interview with Amr ElAfifi, Berlin, May, 2022.

55. Yousuf, interview.

Epilogue

1. Amal, interview with Amr ElAfifi, Berlin, May, 2022.

2. Bessan Kassab and Rana Mamdouh, "Count of the Pardon Committee..The Release of 59 Activists from State Security..and Abu Eita, Some People are Halting Our Efforts" (in Arabic), *Mada Masr*, June 4, 2022, https://www.madamasr.com/ar/2022/06/04/news/u/ناش-59-سبيل-إخلاء-الرئاسي-العفو-حصيلة.

3. Declan Walsh, "Why Was an Italian Graduate Student Tortured and Murdered in Egypt?," *New York Times*, August 15, 2017, https://www.nytimes.com/2017/08/15/magazine/giulio-regeni-italian-graduate-student-tortured-murdered-egypt.html.

4. Sheena Chestnut Greitens, *Dictators and Their Secret Police: Coercive Institutions and State Violence* (Cambridge: Cambridge University Press, 2016).

5. Yousuf, interview.

6. Samir Hosni and Mohamed Abelmajid, "President Sisi to Egyptians: Nothing Stays the Same, and God Is on Our Side" (in Arabic), *Youm Al-Sabe'*. October 13, 2022, https://www.youm7.com/story/2022/10/13/5939310/معاناتا-وربنا-حالها-على-بتفضل-مش-الدنيا-للمصريين-السيسي-الرئيس.

7. Elizabeth R. Nugent, *After Repression* (Princeton, New Jersey: Princeton University Press, 2020).

Lightning Source UK Ltd.
Milton Keynes UK
UKHW050451160223
417096UK00036B/539